Civil Procedure in Finland

Civil Procedure in Finland

Second Edition

Johanna Niemi

This book was originally published as a monograph in the International Encyclopaedia of Laws/Civil Procedure.

General Editors: Roger Blanpain, Frank Hendrickx
Volume Editor: Piet Taelman

Wolters Kluwer

Published by:
Kluwer Law International B.V.
PO Box 316
2400 AH Alphen aan den Rijn
The Netherlands
Website: www.wklawbusiness.com

Sold and distributed in North, Central and South America by:
Wolters Kluwer Legal & Regulatory U.S.
7201 McKinney Circle
Frederick, MD 21704
United States of America
Email: customer.service@wolterskluwer.com

Sold and distributed in all other countries by:
Turpin Distribution Services Ltd.
Stratton Business Park
Pegasus Drive, Biggleswade
Bedfordshire SG18 8TQ
United Kingdom
Email: kluwerlaw@turpin-distribution.com

Printed on acid-free paper

ISBN 978-90-411-6940-2

This title is available on www.kluwerlawonline.com

Printed and Bound by CPI Group (UK) Ltd, Croydon, CR0 4YY.

The Author

Johanna Niemi (Niemi-Kiesiläinen), Professor of Procedural Law, Academy Professor, University of Turku. She received her doctorate in law at University of Helsinki in 1995. She was professor of law at Umeå University in Sweden in 2004–2007 and vice dean (teaching) at University of Helsinki 2010–2013. She was a visiting Fulbright scholar at University of Wisconsin in 1997–1998 and visiting professor at University of Lund 2009–2012.

Niemi has taught criminal and civil procedure, including trial advocacy courses, insolvency law and courses on law and gender. She has written extensively on Finnish and comparative insolvency law, procedural law, human rights and violence against women. She has led several research projects, for example, 'Violence in the Shadow of Equality: Hidden Gender in the Legal Discourse in 2001–2004' and 'Gendered Choices 2013-2015'. She was the co-editor of several journals and books; notably *Responsible Selves. Women in the Nordic Legal Culture* (Ashgate 2001; with Nousiainen, Gunnarsson and Lundström), *Consumer Bankruptcy in Global Perspective* (Hart Publishing 2003; with Iain Ramsay and William Whitford), *Consumer Credit, Debt and Bankruptcy: Comparative and International Perspectives* (Hart Publishing 2009; with Ramsay and Whitford) and *Nordic Equality at a Crossroads. Feminist Legal Studies Coping with Difference* (Ashgate 2004; with Eva-Maria Svensson and Anu Pylkkänen).

The Author

Table of Contents

Acknowledgements

Professor Erkki Havansi first introduced me to this project and I am grateful for his support in this as well as in earlier projects. Erkki Havansi and district court judge Satu Seppänen were co-authors of a paper presented in a conference on provisional measures in Athens in 1998 that was the basis of Part IX Chapter 1. Four sources made my work easier and more pleasant than it would have been otherwise. The book Law of Procedure (in Finnish; WSOY), which has been a common project of several Finnish procedural scholars, was a great help. I am especially indebted to Professor Juha Lappalainen who wrote its chapters on civil procedure and Professor Jyrki Virolainen who wrote about general principles. Professor Antti Jokelas's chapter on the law of procedure in the book *Introduction to Finnish Law* was helpful in finding the English terminology. I have also used the translation of central laws into the English language that can be found in Finlex. Finally, the English language book on Swedish civil procedure by Professor Bengt Lindell helped me to structure the presentation. Students Andreas Philipsson, Johan Högberg and Anna Svedjevik at Umeå University and Tyyni Laiho at University of Turku helped me with the technicalities of the text. Tarja Linden has made the pictures. Head of Department Kari Kiesiläinen read the manuscript and commented on the administration of justice. I wish to thank all of them.

Text Scope Country: Finland

Text Scope Organization: [16. Organization name for Intergovernmental Organizations series (instead of country name)]

List of Abbreviations

ArbA	Arbitration Act (*Laki välimiesmenettelystä* 967/1992)
BA	Bankruptcy Act (*Konkurssilaki* 120/2004)
Child Custody Act	Act on Child Custody and Right of Access (*Laki lapsen huollosta ja tapaamisoikeudesta* 361/1983)
CivMedAct	Act on Mediation in Civil Matters and Confirmation of Settlements in General Courts (*Laki riita-asioiden sovittelusta ja sovinnon vahvistamisesta yleisissä tuomioistuimissa* 394/2011)
Civil Servants Act	The Act on Civil Servants of the State (*Valtion virkamieslaki* 750/1994)
Conciliation Act	Act on Conciliation in Criminal and Certain Civil Cases (Laki sovittelusta rikosasioissa ja eräissä riita-asioissa 1015/2005)
Constitution	The Constitution of Finland (*Suomen perustuslaki* 731/1999)
Court Publicity Act	Act on the Publicity of Court Proceedings in General Courts (*Laki oikeudenkäynnin julkisuudesta yleisissä tuomioistuimissa* 370/2007)
Debt Adjustment Act	Act on the Adjustment of the Debts of a Private Individual (*Laki yksityishenkilön velkajärjestelystä* 57/1993)
ECHR	The European Convention on Human Rights and Fundamental Freedoms 1950
ECtHR	European Court of Human Rights
EU	European Union (referring also to European Communities)
Freedom of Expression Act	Act on the Exercise of Freedom of Expression in Mass Media (*Laki sananvapauden käyttämisestä joukkoviestinnässä* 460/2003)
HE	Government's proposal to the Parliament Bill (*Hallituksen esitys*)

List of Abbreviations

KHO	Supreme Administrative Court
KKO	Supreme Court (*Korkein oikeus*)
OK, Code of Procedure	Code of Judicial Procedure (*Oikeudenkäymiskaari* 4/1734)
Publicity Act	Act on the Openness of Government Activities (*Laki viranomaistoiminnan julkisuudesta* 621/1999)
ROL	Criminal Procedure Act (*Laki oikeudenkäynnistä rikosasioissa* 689/1997)
TFEU	Treaty on the Functioning of the European Union
UK	Enforcement Code (*Ulosottokaari* 705/2007)

Note 1: Unauthorized translations of many laws are found at ⟨www.finlex.fi/en/laki/kaannokset⟩
Note 2: The Finnish language has only one pronoun (*hän*) for she and he. In this presentation I have made an attempt to avoid personal pronouns as much as possible and repeat words like plaintiff and defendant. When it has not been possible, I use *he* for the plaintiff, *she* for the defendant, and *she* for others.

General Introduction

§1. General Background

1. Finland made a proclamation of independence in 1917 and after a short but bloody civil war in 1918 the new State enacted its first Constitution in 1919. The Constitution, which remained in force until 1999, was based on democratic principles of government. As a multiparty democratic State, with a population of 5.5 million, Finland joined the Council of Europe in 1989 and the European Union (EU) in 1995. Finland also joined the Euro in 2002.

2. Finland has a democratic government and a multiparty system. The President of the Republic is elected in direct ballot every six years.

3. Typically for the multiparty system, there are usually several parties in the government. Historically, the main partners in the coalition have been two out of three: the Conservatives, The Centre and the Social Democrats. As none of the parties can expect to have a majority and to govern alone, the politics tend to seek consensus among the parties. About the history and politics of Finland see ⟨http://virtual.finland.fi⟩.

4. Finland is a unitary State and has no federal structure. The State government at the regional level (*lääninhallitukset; since 2010 aluehallintovirasto AVI Regional State Administrative Authority http://www.avi.fi/en/web/avi-en/#.VO20400cSUk*) has no representative or elected body. The State also has other regional authorities such as ELY: Centres for Economic Development, Transport and the Environment (http://www.ely-keskus.fi/en/web/ely-en/). In addition, the police, the prosecutor and the execution officer are organized in regional units. Also, the municipalities have created regional coalitions (*maakuntaliitot*) to carry out advanced tasks such as central hospitals and vocational schools. The regional level of governing is under lively political debate in 2016 because the municipalities cannot bear the burden of health and social care anymore. It is uncertain at the moment what the new regional structure will look like in the future.

5. The local communities have a certain degree of self-government with democratically elected city and rural municipality councils (*kunnan- ja kaupunginvaltuustot*). The local communities have self-government and appoint their own directors and employees. The communities also collect local taxes to finance their government. In practice, however, the tasks of the communities in the fields of education, health care and social services are today regulated by national laws and financed through State budget. During the 2010s, several municipalities have merged, the number of municipalities has gone down (313 in 2016) and the average population of municipalities has increased (17,000 in 2015) (http://www.localfinland.fi/en/authorities/Pages/default.aspx). Discussions about the reform of the local administration abound. The number of municipalities is still considered high and since the size of the communities varies from less than 1,000 inhabitants up over 600.000 in the capital, Helsinki, it is difficult to provide equal services in all parts of the country.

6. Freedom of religion is guaranteed in Article 11 of the Constitution. Most Finns (73% of the population at the end of the year 2015) belong to the Evangelic Lutheran church, which has a legally regulated status and collects the church fees through the national tax collection system (Church Law; *Kirkkolaki* 1054/1993). Also the Orthodox Church enjoys a privileged status according to the Law on the Orthodox Church (*Laki ortodoksisesta kirkosta* 985/2006). The public schools have religion in their curricula. The students have the right to choose slightly confessional evangelic or orthodox studies or non-religious ethical studies. Also, education in other religions is organized at the request of three or more students.

7. Finland was part of the Swedish monarchy since medieval times until Finland was annexed to Russia in 1809. Due to historical reasons, the country has two national languages, Finnish and Swedish (The Constitution of Finland § 17.1–2 (731/1999)). While over 90% of the population are native Finnish speakers, about 5% speak Swedish as their first language. Because Swedish is an official language, all laws and bills are translated to Swedish. They are available in print and at <www.riksdagen.fi> and <www.finlex.fi>. The school curriculum favours the Swedish language, which was a mandatory school subject until 2004. Everyone has the right to use their own language, Finnish or Swedish, before the courts and other authorities, and to receive decisions and documents in that language. The Language Act (*Kielilaki* 423/2003) gives the detailed provisions on this right. It is supplemented by the Act on the Knowledge of the Languages Required of Personnel in Public Bodies (*Laki julkisyhteisöjen henkilöstöltä vaadittavasta kielitaidosta* 424/2003).

8. The indigenous Sami population of about 5,000 members has some degree of self-government in the Northern parts of Finland. The rights of the Sami, the Roma and other groups to maintain and develop their language and culture are acknowledged in the Constitution (§ 17.3). The Sami population has a right to use its own language in the courts and administrative bodies in the northern parts of the country (Sámi Language Act; *Saamen kielilaki* 1086/2003).The Russian minority is the largest of the other language groups. They largely emigrated from Russia in the 1990s and many of them have ancestors who had a connection with Finland.

9. Due to the common history, the Finnish legal system has a lot in common with the Swedish one. Even during the Russian rule (1809–1917), Finland was allowed to keep most of the Swedish laws in force. After independence in 1917, the Finns have followed the Swedes in many legal issues. After World War II, the Nordic legal cooperation led to the ratification of a number of Nordic treaties in international private and procedural law. In addition, some degree of harmonization was achieved in commercial law and other fields of law (generally about the Finnish legal system see Hollo (ed.) 2006; Pöyhönen (ed.) 2002; Nuotio, Melander & Huomo-Kettunen (eds) 2012).

10. The Finnish Constitution of 1999 makes a distinction between legislative, governmental and judicial powers. The Constitutional Law Committee of the Parliament is vested with the task of controlling the conformity of the Acts of the Parliament with the Constitution (The Constitution of Finland § 74; *Suomen perustuslaki* 731/1999). The opinions of the Constitutional Law Committee on the Bills are prepared with a thorough hearing of experts in constitutional law and they are regarded as important sources of constitutional law.

11. According to the Constitution, the independent courts exercise the judicial powers and the Supreme Court and the Supreme Administrative Court are the highest instances (Constitution § 3). The legislative powers are vested in Parliament. The courts have no role in legislative processes, but the President of the State may obtain a statement from the Supreme Court before confirming an Act (Constitution § 77). This power is rarely used. The highest courts may also submit a proposal to the government if they find a legislative initiative necessary (Constitution § 99). Since the new Constitution came into force in 1999, the courts also exercise constitutional control. According to § 106 of the new Constitution, the courts should not apply a law that is in apparent conflict with the Constitution.

12. The administration of the courts is largely based on the principle of self-management. Certain administrative and budgetary functions are, however, organized in the departments of the Ministry of Justice (see Chapter 1, § 1 V).

§2. Delimitation of the Subject Matter

I. Definition of the Term 'Civil Procedure'

13. There is no clear definition of civil procedure in the Finnish legislation. The civil procedure is followed in the general courts in proceedings concerning civil matters, including cases in commercial and consumer disputes, damages, real estate and family matters. The rules of civil procedure are also followed in certain other courts, which adjudicate matters of private or commercial law nature, unless special procedural rules have been enacted. The term civil procedure also covers arbitration and mediation procedures within the courts.

14. The district courts make a number of decisions that can be characterized as judicial supervision (*jurisdictio voluntaria*), including appointment of the executor of the estate of a deceased person or of a legal guardian. If such matters are undisputed, the special rules of Chapter 8 of the Code of Procedure are followed (Part VIII, Chapters 2 and 3). If there appears to be a dispute in the matter, general rules of civil procedure apply. Also, appeals against the decisions of enforcement agencies are made to district courts (Part IX). The district courts also handle insolvency cases (Part VIII, Chapter 4). Adjudication in debt enforcement and insolvency cases is included under the concept of civil procedure.

II. Distinction with Other Types of Procedure

15. Until 1997, when the Criminal Procedure Act (*Laki oikeudenkäynnistä rikosasioissa* 689/1997) was enacted, the civil and criminal procedures were both regulated in the Code of Procedure and they shared many common paragraphs. After the reform, the regulations were separated but the two procedure forms still share certain general principles. Today, the law on evidence and appeal are still regulated in the same chapters of the Code of Procedure for both types of procedure.

16. The civil and criminal matters are adjudicated by the same courts and, often, even by the same chambers. In certain situations, matters of a private law nature are adjudicated in the criminal proceedings. Especially damages and other civil claims based on a crime can be adjudicated together with the crime in the criminal proceeding (ROL 3:1). If the criminal charge is dismissed, the compensation claim can be adjudicated according to the rules of the civil procedure (ROL 3:6).

III. Separate Court Systems and Procedures

17. According to the Constitution, the judicial adjudication is basically divided into two jurisdictions, the general and the administrative. The general courts have jurisdiction over civil, commercial and criminal matters and the administrative courts have jurisdiction over the administrative matters (Constitution §§ 98–99). The Constitution also mentions the High Court of Impeachment, which is a special criminal court for the trials against the highest civil servants and judges. In addition, some special courts exist and their jurisdiction is regulated in respective laws (see Chapter 1 and Part II, Chapter 1 § 1).

18. The administrative courts are divided into the Administrative Courts at the regional level and the Supreme Administrative Court. The procedures in the administrative courts are regulated in the Administrative Judicial Procedure Act (*Hallintolainkäyttölaki* 586/1996; an early account of the differences see Lager 1990). The administrative courts have jurisdiction over appeals from decisions of administrative authorities, such as the local government, other local decision-making bodies, the State government and other bodies vested with public power. Also, disputes between administrative authorities or between a private party and an administrative authority can be processed in administrative courts. Thus, the administrative courts process almost all disputes that concern the use of public power.

19. The Supreme Court settles conflicts of jurisdiction between the general courts and the administrative courts. There have been no great controversies over jurisdiction. One possible source of confusion was that the general courts have jurisdiction over cases involving the use of public power whenever an individual seeks compensation or demands criminal responsibility for an action or decision that was caused or committed in the use of public power (Suviranta, 2005). This jurisdiction is stipulated in the Constitution § 118, 3.

§3. Sources of Civil Procedure Law

I. The Constitution and International Law

20. Access to courts and the right to a fair trial are guaranteed in § 21 of the Constitution. More specifically, the paragraph mentions the access to a court or other appropriate body within reasonable time, the right to be heard, the right to a public handling of the case, the right to hear the reasons for a decision and the right to appeal.

21. Finland is since 1976 party to the International Convention on Civil and Political Rights (1966) and since 1990 party to the European Convention on Human Rights (1951). Both conventions guarantee access to the courts and a right to a fair and public hearing within a reasonable time.

22. The European Court of Human Rights has given a number of judgments against Finland in matters concerning the length of the trial.

23. As a member of the EU since 1995, Finland, and Finnish courts in particular, are bound by the EU legal system. According to the Article 81 of the Treaty on the Functioning of the European Union, judicial cooperation concerning civil matters that have cross-border implications and measures that are necessary for the proper functioning of the internal market fall under the competence of the EU. The EU law instruments in the field of civil procedure have been since 2009, when the Lisbon Treaty entered into force, Regulations and, thus, directly applicable in the Member States.[1]

1. For example, Council Regulation (EC) No. 1215/2012 on jurisdiction and the recognition and enforcement of judgments in civil and commercial matters; Regulation (EC) No. 805/2004 of the European Parliament and of the Council of 21 Apr. 2004 creating a European Enforcement Order for uncontested claims; Council Regulation (EC) No. 2201/2003 concerning jurisdiction and the recognition and enforcement of judgments in matrimonial matters and the matters of parental responsibility, repealing Regulation (EC) No. 1347/2000; Council Regulation (EC) No. 1348/2000 on the service in the Member States of judicial and extrajudicial documents in civil or commercial matters; Council Regulation (EC) No. 1206/2001 on cooperation between the courts of the Member States in the taking of evidence in civil or commercial matters.

II. Code of Procedure

24. Finland has a civil law tradition. The legislative powers lie with the Parliament and the acts of Parliament play a major role in the legislation. The Parliament can delegate powers to promulgate degrees to the Finnish State President, to the government or to the ministries (Constitution § 80). Since the rights and duties of the individuals are regulated by acts of Parliament, the degrees play a minor role in the regulation of civil procedure. However, detailed provisions on the courts and the competencies of the judges are regulated by degrees (paragraph 30 below).

25. The civil procedure is regulated in the Code of Judicial Procedure (*Oikeudenkäymiskaari* 4/1734). The Code of Procedure was originally enacted as part of the Swedish Code of 1734. When Finland was annexed to Russia in 1809, Swedish legislation largely remained in force. The Code of Procedure survived the Russian rule of 1809–1917. After Finland became independent in 1917, the Code of Procedure continued to exist and today the civil procedure is still formally regulated by the same Code, even though only a few paragraphs have their original content and wording.

26. During the twentieth century, several partial reforms were carried out. Most importantly, the rules of evidence were reformed in 1948. Legal aid was introduced in 1955 and has been amended several times. The rules on extraordinary review were changed in 1960 and the right of appeal to the Supreme Court was restricted in 1979. The basic structures of the court system and the civil and criminal procedures, however, remained intact until the 1990s.

27. During the twentieth century, several comprehensive reform proposals were prepared. The first proposal of 1903, presented by a committee headed by Professor R.A. Wrede, already contained most of the principles that carried the day in the final reforms by the end of the century. Some of the later proposals were delayed because of the World Wars. In the 1970s, the position and recruitment of the judges became an object of heated political controversy that effectively delayed the reform plans for more than a decade.

28. In the 1980s, the reform plans took wind again in a more neutral atmosphere. The structure of the district courts was finally confirmed by Parliament in 1987 and the historical difference between city courts and rural courts was abolished. The civil procedure in the first instance courts was completely reformed in 1991. Several new chapters were added to the Code of Procedure (Chapter 5 on summons and preparation of the trial; Chapter 6 on main hearing; Chapter 7 on injunctions; Chapter 9 on pleadings; Chapter 18 on joinder, etc.). Both reforms entered into force on 1 December 1993. At the same time, an additional reform Act on legal expenses (Chapter 21 of the Code of Procedure) entered into force. In 1997, the criminal procedure was reformed and a separate Criminal Procedure Act was enacted. At the same time, some adjustments to the Code of Procedure were made (about the reform see Ervo 1995; Niemi-Kiesiläinen 2008; about the civil procedure in English see Jokela 2002). The legal literature on procedural law has been quite rich after the reforms of the 1990s. A short list of the literature in Finnish is included at the end of the monograph.

29. Furthermore, the procedure in the appeal courts was reformed in 1998. Before the reform, the procedure in appeal courts was largely based on documents. The appeal courts very rarely heard the parties or witnesses in person. After the 1998 reform, the appeal courts were obliged to hold a hearing and to hear the witnesses or the parties if they were to change the decision due to reconsideration of the orally given evidence. The reform turned out to be extremely difficult to enforce and in 2003 the appeal court procedure was changed again, this time to curtail full hearings of cases that were obviously correctly decided by the district courts. Again, the appeal procedure was reformed in 2011 and in 2015 to implement a more comprehensive system of leave of appeal (Part IV, Chapter 4, § 2 I).

30. The Code of Procedure contains the most important rules on civil procedure. It is complemented by a few additional acts, for example, the Act on the Publicity of the Court Proceedings (*Laki oikeudenkäynnin julkisuudesta* 370/2007; first by Law 945/1984). After the big procedural reforms of the 1990s, the first decade of the twenty-first century was a time of consolidation. A review of the reform was made in 2001, leading to some amendments (768/2002), the most important of which was the new procedure for application matters (jurisdictio voluntaria).

31. The judicial institutions are regulated in separate Acts. The Code of Procedure is complemented by Acts on the organization and administration of the district courts, the appeal courts and the Supreme Court (The District Court Act *Käräjäoikeuslaki* 581/1993; the Court of Appeal Act *Hovioikeuslaki* 56/1994 and the Supreme Court Act *Laki korkeimmasta oikeudesta* 665/2005). In addition, provisions on the organization of the courts is found in Decrees of the government. In February 2016, a Bill to reform the regulation of the courts, concentrate the rules in one Act on the Courts and to abolish the decrees has been introduced in the Parliament (HE 7/2017), with the aim of having it in force in 2017.[2] In addition, important acts on civil procedure are, for example, the Advocates Act (*Laki asianajajista* 496/1958), the Legal Aid Offices Act (*Laki valtion oikeusaputoimistoista* 258/2002) and the Bailiffs' Act (*Haastemieslaki* 505/1986), Act on the European Enforcement Order for Uncontested Claims (*Laki riitauttamattomia vaatimuksia koskevasta eurooppalaisesta täytäntöönpanoperusteesta* 825/2005), Act on a European Small Claims Procedure (*Laki eurooppalaisesta vähäisiin vaatimuksiin sovellettavasta menettelystä* 753/2008) implementing Regulation 1896/2006 and Act on a European Order for Payment Procedure (*Laki eurooppalaisesta maksamismääräysmenettelystä* 754/2008) implementing Regulation 861/2007 as well as the Arbitration Act (*Laki välimiesmenettelystä 967*/1992).

2. Ministry of Justice: Mietintöjä ja lausuntoja 26/2014: Uusi tuomioistuinlaki: http://www.oikeusministerio.fi/fi/index/julkaisut/julkaisuarkisto/1397739494559.html.

III. Generally about Sources of Law

32. In the Finnish doctrine on the sources of the law, Professor Aulis Aarnio distinguished between strongly binding, weakly binding and allowed sources of law. He includes law, systematic arguments and customary law in the first group. Customary law is also mentioned in one of the few original articles of the Code of Procedure that have not been changed since 1734. According to Article 1:11 '[I]n the absence of statutory law, the custom of the land, if not unreasonable, shall also be her guide.' In the interpretation of procedural law, however, customary law plays a small role.

33. Instead, case law of the Supreme Court is an important source of law. The precedents of the Supreme Court are not considered legally binding on the lower courts. The doctrine holds that the case law of the Supreme Court has a weakly binding force, that is, the lower courts are obliged to follow the precedents but, in case they find reason to deviate from a precedent, they can do so but are obliged to give the reasoning for doing so. In practice, however, the precedents of the Supreme Court are very highly respected in the practice of the lower courts.

34. The Supreme Court quite actively delivers precedents in procedural issues. The activity of the Court is related to frequent changes in procedural legislation, the interpretation of which has often required guidance from the Supreme Court. The interaction has also gone the other way. Some of the changes were preceded by case law. For example, the requirement to hold a hearing in the Court of Appeal was first recognized in the precedents of the Supreme Court and later confirmed by the amendments of the Code of Procedure.

35. The preparatory works warrant some caution as to sources of law in the doctrine. According to the Code of Procedure 1:11 '[A] judge shall carefully examine the true purpose and grounds for the law and render judgment accordingly, and not following her own opinions against the law.' Thus, the judge is trusted with the task of finding and understanding the purpose of the law and of using it as a primary guide in interpretation. In practice, the statements in the *travaux preparatoires*, especially in the Bills of the government, include important information about the intended purposes and interpretation of the laws.

36. The general principles have been frequently discussed in the legal theory (Jonkka 1991; Leppänen 1998; Ervo 2005; Nylund 2006; etc.). The theory makes a distinction between legal rules and legal principles. The former are rules of law that can be applied directly in a case, whereas the latter are principles that can be balanced against each other and be implemented in accordance with their weight as compared with opposing principles. While rules are usually found in the written law (or exceptionally in other sources of law), the principles sometimes find expression in written law, for example in constitutional and human rights, but often they are articulated in the literature of scholars or in the case law on the basis of indirect institutional support.

§4. General Features of the Administration of Justice in Civil Matters

I. Characteristics of the Procedure

37. General principles traditionally played a role in procedural law and scholars have discussed the principles at length. The development of legal theory led to a re-evaluation of the principles of procedural law. Several young scholars started to derive the principles of procedural law from the constitutional and human rights principles.

38. The civil procedure is adversarial and guided by *the principle of party disposition*. The principle of party disposition entails that the parties have the right and the duty to present the claims, the legal grounds and the evidence in a civil trial. The court is bound by the claims and the legal grounds that the party has presented in a case that can be settled by a contract between the parties outside the trial (dispositive cases). In the application of the law, meaning the legal characterization of the matter, the principle of party disposition does not have similar binding force on the court. Instead, the *jura novit curia* principle is followed, meaning that the court is not bound by the legal characterization made by the parties. The court should, however, inform the parties if it has another opinion of the relevant law or correct application of the law than the one presented by the parties.

39. In the law of evidence, the *principle of material truth* has high regard. Several scholars make a distinction between procedural truth and material truth. While the procedural truth only approximates the material truth, the pursuit for a decision that is based on correct fact-finding is highly valued. In addition, the principle of free preponderance of evidence is followed. During trial, the parties are responsible for presenting the evidence. According to the law (OK 17:7), the court has certain powers to call new evidence even in civil cases but in practice the courts hardly ever use these powers (Part VII).

40. In the recent scholarly discussion on the procedural principles, a distinction between the principles related to fair trial and the principles related to the organization of the trial is made. The traditional leading principles of the organization of the trial, according to late Professor Tauno Tirkkonen, were (legal) security, speed and cost-effectiveness. The concept of security here refers to the material truth, which has always been in high regard. With the human rights principles, *the right to a trial within a reasonable time*, a new meaning is given to the old principle of speed or fast trial. The cost-effectiveness seems to have lost its status as a legal principle but it certainly is a factor regarded in the reforms of the court administration and procedure. Recently, Professor Jyrki Virolainen has made a more nuanced differentiation among the principles. He includes (legal) security, procedural efficiency and equality in the group of principles of value and purpose. As specific groups of principles he distinguishes the procedural principles of orality, concentration and immediacy and the role principles that guide the division of tasks and powers between the judge and the parties.

41. The powers of the judge to administer a case are conceptualized under the concept *of formal direction of the process*. After the 1993 reform, the judge is responsible for the organization of the trial so that the main hearing can be continuous and immediate. The judge has powers to set deadlines and govern the process accordingly.

42. During the 1993 reform, the process was streamlined in two distinct phases, *the preparatory stage and the main hearing*. The purpose of the preparation stage is to facilitate the trial, in other words, the main hearing. The main hearing should be held in one continuous oral hearing, in which all the evidence should be presented immediately to the judge or a panel that gives the verdict based on the material presented in the main hearing. The *principles of orality, concentration and immediacy* of the main hearing were the leading principles of the reform. The reform has turned out to be very successful. The main hearings are generally arranged according to the above-mentioned principles. This has been achieved by a detailed regulation of the preparatory stage and fairly rigorous use of preclusion rules (see Männistö 2013). The preparatory stage has been prolonged in a number of cases, however on the negative side, we also have to take into account the unanticipated rise in the costs of litigation. In 2002, the review of the reform led to some amendments of the Code, the purpose of which was to make procedure more flexible.

II. Fundamental Guarantees

43. The principle of fair trial and access to a court are guaranteed in § 21 of the Constitution. More specifically, the paragraph mentions the access to a court or other appropriate body within reasonable time, the right to be heard, the right to a public handling of the case, the right to hear the reasons for a decision and the right to appeal. Since the constitutional article is concise, the ECHR Article 6 and the case law of the ECtHR complement. *The independence and impartiality of the judges* is one of the fundamental principles of Finnish constitutional law.

44. The right *to a fair and public hearing within a reasonable time* has been an issue in the European Court of Human Rights several times. The ECtHR has given a number of judgments in cases against Finland concerning the length of the trial in criminal cases (e.g., *Lehtonen et al. v. Finland* 13.6.2006; *Hopotihoi & Kangasluoma v. Finland* 22.9.2009; *Toive Lehtinen v. Finland* 31.3.2009 and 22.5.2007; *Sorvisto v. Finland* 13.1.2009; *Ahlskog v. Finland* 13.11.2008). In civil procedure, the length of a case concerning paternity and access to the child has been found to be too long in *Nuutinen v. Finland* 27.6.2000. The delay of a trial can be compensated according to Act on Compensation for Delay of Trial (*Laki oikeudenkäynnin viivästyksen hyvittämisestä* 362/2009). The Act regulates claims towards the State. The Act entered into force 1 January 2010 and compensation can be claimed in cases that are pending after that date (§ 14). Compensation can be claimed during the trial at the district court or appeal court before the proceedings on the main issue have been ended (§ 7). The upper limit of compensation is EUR 10,000 and a standard is EUR 1,500 for each year that the suit has been delayed because of the omission or action that the State is responsible for (§ 6).

45. The contradictory principle always was one of the fundamental principles of Finnish law of procedure. During the last ten years, its importance is emphasized in the case law of ECtHR concerning Finland and in the legal doctrine. Tatu Leppänen (1998), Sakari Laukkanen (1995), Mika Huovila (2003) and Laura Ervo (2005) extended the scope of the principle from a purely formal one to one that encompasses the rights to fair trial and to fair opportunity to present one's arguments. The European Court of Human Rights (ECtHR) has also found that Finland has violated the contradictory principle when all evidence had not been communicated to the opposing party *(K.S. v. Finland* 31.5.2001; *K.P. v. Finland* 31.5.2001; *M.S. v. Finland* 22.3.2005, a criminal case).The contradictory principle is complemented by *the principle of equality* (Constitution § 6). The equality of arms is reflected both in the requirement that the court treats both parties in an equal manner and in the availability of and right to legal aid (Part VI, Chapter 2).

46. The principle of the public trial has traditionally been respected in the general courts and it is encompassed in the Act on the Publicity of Court Proceedings in General Courts (*Laki oikeudenkäynnin julkisuudesta yleisissä tuomioistuimissa* 370/2007) that replaced the Act of 1984 (945/1984). Until the late 1990s, the hearings were usually held in public and the procedural materials were freely available for reading and copying. The rare exceptions were criminal proceedings involving State security interest or under-age defendants. In 1997, the ECtHR held that Finland had violated the right to privacy when the medical report of a witness had become public at a trial (ECtHR *Z v. Finland*, 25 February 1997), and the old regime has been replaced by a more nuanced regulation (Act on the Publicity of Court Proceedings in General Courts; *Laki oikeudenkäynnin julkisuudesta yleisissä tuomioistuimissa* 370/2007 and Act on the Openness of Government Activities; *Laki viranomaistoiminnan julkisuudesta* 621/1999). The purposes of the new Act in 2007 were to emphasize the publicity of the trial as a basic principle, to give the courts more case-by-case discretion, and to facilitate open trials in cases in which some part of the evidence is confidential (HE 13/2007).

47. The basic principle is that the trials in general courts are public. In a civil procedure the court may order a hearing to be held behind closed doors if a public hearing would endanger the security interests or foreign relations of the State, reveal sensitive information about the private life, health, disability or social welfare of individuals or put an asylum seeker at risk (Court Publicity Act § 15). The court may order a hearing behind closed doors if matters that are confidential according to other laws are to be revealed (§ 10). In addition, a hearing can be held behind closed doors partially or wholly if a document is presented or a fact is revealed as an exception to the rules of confidentiality or a person younger than 15 years is heard. The court records and evidentiary documents are also generally open to public. Documents including information that is relevant to state security or foreign relations or concerning privacy are confidential information unless the court decides otherwise.

The court may also order other documents containing legally protected information to be kept secret. The period of secrecy is twenty-five, sixty or eighty years. The deliberations of the court are always confidential (§ 23). The decisions are public. The judgment and the relevant provisions of law are always public. Parts of the reasoning of the judgment can be declared confidential as far as they contain confidential information. In such cases, a public report of the decision shall be made (§ 25). However, the deliberations of the court are confidential (OK 1:7; KKO:2002:27; KKO:1998:134; KKO:1998:35).

Part I. Judicial Organization

Chapter 1. The Courts and Their Members

§1. COURTS

I. Structure of the Court System

48. The court system is divided into the general courts and the administrative courts. In addition, a few other courts have a specifically defined jurisdiction over certain group of matters.

Figure 1

The Finnish Court System

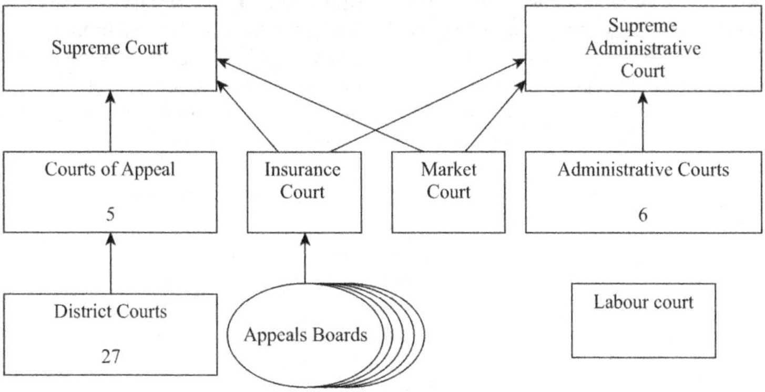

49. The general courts are the District courts in the first instance, the Appeal Courts and the Supreme Court. The number of district courts declined when bigger court units were formed and there are now (2016) twenty-seven district courts and six appeal courts.

50. The administrative courts are six Administrative Courts at the regional level and the Supreme Administrative Court. The procedures in the administrative courts are regulated in the Administrative Judicial Procedure Act. The administrative courts have jurisdiction over appeals from decisions of administrative authorities, most notably of local government and other local decision-making bodies and of State government, and other bodies vested with public power. Also, disputes between administrative authorities or between a private party and an administrative authority can be processed in administrative courts. Thus, the administrative courts handle almost all disputes that involve the use of public power (about the court system, see Vilkkonen 1985).

51. The general courts have jurisdiction over cases involving the use of public power when an individual seeks damages or demands criminal responsibility for an action or decision that has been caused or committed in the use of public power. This jurisdiction is stipulated in the Constitution § 118.3.

52. The specialization of modern society led to the establishment of special courts in the mid-twentieth century. Now the trend has been reversed and the policy is to channel all or most of the civil and criminal matters to ordinary courts. The most obvious evidence of the new policy has been the abolishment of water and land courts in 2000 and 2001 respectively. Their jurisdiction in civil and criminal matters was transferred to district courts. Today only the Labour Court, the Market Court and the Insurance Court have jurisdiction in civil matters. Their jurisdiction is explained in Part II, Chapter 1, § 1 *infra.*

53. Besides the courts, several boards make decisions on matters that fall within the field of civil law in the broad meaning of the word. Some of these boards, for example the Accident Insurance Appeals Board (the Employment Accidents Act (*Tapaturmavakuutuslaki* 608/1948)), make decisions that are legally binding on the parties and which can be enforced. Usually, however, the boards only give recommendations on the interpretation of the law and the compensation level. These recommendations can, however, have important authoritative power in the respective field. A proceeding with such a board does not rule out an action in the district court in the same matter. In a subsequent action in the court, the decision of the board can be replaced but, since the boards are often specialized in the respective field, the courts often observe their decisions. Examples of such boards are the Consumer Complaints Board, the jurisdiction of which is discussed later in Part II, Chapter 1, the Complaints Board for Patient Injuries (the Patient Injury Act (*Potilasvahinkolaki* 585/1986) and the Complaints Board for Traffic Injuries (*Laki liikennevahinkolautakunnasta* 441/2002). Also worth mentioning are the boards that were set up by a branch itself, such as the Insurance Board and the Council for Mass Media. Even though these boards only give recommendations to firms in the respective fields, their decisions are mostly followed (more about the boards, see Rosti et al. 2008).

A. *District Courts*

54. Until 1993, the district courts were organized differently in towns and in rural areas. Historically, the towns supported their own courthouses (*raastuvanoikeus; rådstuvurätt*) and the town council selected its own judges. The panel of three judges consisted of two legally trained judges and one lay judge, who usually had full time service in the court. The courts (*kihlakunnanoikeus; häradsrätt*) in the countryside had large jurisdictional areas and the chief judge often travelled long distances to hold the hearings of the court. The judge was regularly replaced by clerks, young lawyers who completed their university training with one year of practice in the court. The court had a quorum consisting of one judge and a panel of seven lay judges. The lay judges were local representatives of the public selected by the local council and served only on the days when the court had a hearing in their locality. The seven lay members had a common vote and they could vote down the judge only when unanimous. This outdated system sustained with minor modifications in the Code of 1734 until 1993.

55. In the 1993 reform, the regulation of district courts was unified and the historical difference between city courts and rural courts was abolished. In the 1990s and 2000s a number of district courts have been merged and their total number is twenty-seven in 2016 (Law 1751/2009; HE 227/2009; reforming the District Court Act 581/1993). The biggest district court is the District Court of Helsinki with almost 100 judges. The chief judge of the district court who has a historical title *laamanni* has administrative responsibility for the court. The larger district courts are divided into departments. The district court judges *(käräjätuomari)* are independent in their judicial discretion.

B. Appellate Courts

56. Six Courts of Appeal handle the appeals from district courts. They also have a certain administrative and supervising function concerning the district courts. The Courts of Appeal are in Turku (founded in 1623), Vaasa (founded in 1776), Kuopio (Appeal Court for Eastern Finland, founded in Viipuri 1839), Helsinki (founded in 1952), and Rovaniemi (founded in 1979). The Appeal court in Kouvola (founded in 1979) has been merged with the Appeal Court of Eastern Finland in 2014 (Law 281/2013).

C. The Supreme Court

57. The Supreme Court handles the appeals from the Courts of Appeal and certain other courts. It has the power to make final decisions over issues of jurisdiction between ordinary and administrative courts or special courts. It also has some administrative powers and supervisory functions over the lower courts and enforcement authorities (Constitution § 99).

58. The most important task of the Supreme Court is to give judgments with a precedent value in appeal cases. Therefore, the Supreme Court only takes up a case after it has been granted a leave. The leave is required in all appeal cases from the appeal courts and in some other cases as well. The leave is granted approximately in 10% of the cases. The precedents are published and the number of published cases varies between 100 and 150 cases per year.

59. The Supreme Court sits in Helsinki. Its chief justice is called President of the Supreme Court. In the period 2006–2015, the President was Pauliine Koskelo and since 2016 Timo Esko. The Supreme Court has at least fifteen members (the Supreme Court Act § 10).

II. Administration of the Court

60. The administration of the courts is divided between the courts themselves and the Ministry of Justice. The Department of Judicial Administration of the ministry is responsible for the allocation of the resources of the courts, the development of the justice system and education of the judges. In the allocation of resources, the management of results is followed, that is, the courts and the ministry follow the planning and output of the respective court in annual negotiations. The ministry is not involved in the appointment of the judges after the establishment of a special appointment board for the judges (the Act on Judicial Appointments (*Laki tuomareiden nimittämisestä* 205/2000). The courts themselves carry out their internal administration.

III. Bench

A. District Courts

61. The district courts have a different quorum in civil and criminal matters. The role of the lay judges has been diminished and they do not appear in civil proceedings any longer. In civil cases, the basic quorum in a main hearing is three judges. If the full quorum is not necessary because of the nature of the case and neither party requests it, the main hearing can be held before a court consisting of only one judge. This judge is always the one who has responsibility for the preparation of the case (OK 2:5). This rule has had the somewhat unintended consequence that one judge is by far the most common composition of the district court in the main hearing. The full quorum of three judges is only used in about 4% of the cases.

62. The quorum is one judge in application matters that are not transferred to ordinary civil proceedings. Application matters include divorce, non-disputed child custody cases, insolvency proceedings etc. Also civil injunctions are decided by one judge alone. The preparation of a case is always the responsibility of a sole judge who is a member of the court in the main hearing (OK 2:5.1 p 2). This judge will chair the preparatory hearings. The summary cases, that is debt enforcement cases, are almost always decided in written proceedings.

63. In summary cases the competence has been delegated to assisting staff, such as permanent assistant judges (*käräjäviskaali*; District Court Act § 3a–3b), court clerks during their one year traineeship (*käräjänotaari;* District Court Act § 4; §§ 14–17) and secretarial staff of the court (District Court Act § 19). The competence of the assistant judges and court clerks, who have a legal education, is similarly regulated: They can adjudicate summary cases and application matters and sit as members of the panel of three judges. The secretarial staff members can give default judgments in summary cases and make decisions in non-fault divorce matters.

B. Appeal Courts

64. The appeal courts do not have jurisdiction in the first instance in civil matters. In certain matters of international family law, such as returning a child who has been unlawfully moved to Finland, the Court of Appeal makes decisions as the first instance. The process according to the Hague Convention of 25 October 1980 on the Civil Aspects of International Child Abduction is regulated in the Act on Child Custody and Right of Access (*Laki lapsen huollosta ja tapaamisoikeudesta* 361/1983 § 31 as amended by the Law 186/1994).

65. In some criminal matters, the appeal courts have jurisdiction in the first instance. Such matters are prosecutions against district court judges and certain other civil servants in the court system and prosecutors. (The jurisdiction for high treason was transferred from the appeal court to the District Court of Helsinki by ROL 4: 4a, as amended by the Law 667/2005).

66. The chief judge of the appeal court is called President of the Appeal Court. The court is divided into sections and the chiefs of sections have the prestigious title *laamanni*.

67. The appeal courts have a quorum of three judges. A case can also be decided in a plenary or in a panel of seven judges, but this rarely happens. The judges lead the preparation of the case and have certain powers to make decisions in a quorum of one judge. For example, one judge may decide on injunctions, leave of appeal and legal aid (OK 2:8; the Court of Appeal Act §§ 8–9).

C. The Supreme Court

68. The quorum of the Supreme Court is five justices. Most important cases may be decided in a plenary or in a quorum of eleven justices. The leave of appeal to the Supreme Court is granted or rejected in a quorum of three justices (OK 2:9; 666/2005).

IV. Appointment of Judges

69. The President of the Republic appoints all tenured judges after the government has presented a candidate (the Act on Judicial Appointments).

70. The chief justices of the Supreme and Supreme Administrative Court are appointed without a formal preparatory procedure. The justices of the Supreme and Supreme Administrative Court are appointed after the respective Court has selected a candidate and has forwarded the proposal to the government. The opening of a position is announced and the candidates can declare interest in the office to the Court.

71. Judges of other courts are appointed after the office of the judge is announced publicly and the appointment procedure is regulated in the Act on Judicial Appointments. An independent body, the Judge Appointment Board, is established for the preparation of the nominations. This board has twelve members, nine of whom represent the judges of different courts, one represents the advocates, one represents the prosecutors and one represents the law faculties. The board assesses the candidates, based on the competence criteria, which are explained *supra* at § 2, and presents its proposal to the government and the President.

72. As a general rule, judges are appointed for tenure. A judge can be appointed for a fixed term to replace a permanent judge during a leave of absence or for other special reasons, such as a temporary overload of cases. The President of the Republic also appoints justices to the Supreme Court for a fixed term. Other appointments for a fixed term are made by the Court itself or by a higher court.

73. Before the final appointment, a candidate for the position as a judge must make a declaration of interests, according to the regulation of civil servants (The Act on Civil Servants of the State (*Valtion virkamieslaki* 750/1994) § 8a (604/1997)).

§2. Members of the Judiciary

I. Competence

A. The Judge

74. The general competence of the judge is stipulated in the Act on Judicial Appointments (§ 11). The judge has to be a Finnish citizen and must hold a degree in law from a Finnish university. The law degree required is at the Master level.[3] Furthermore, the judge must have excellent qualifications in the language of the

3. Before 2005, the master level degree in law was called Candidate of Law, and thus fulfils the qualification for a judge. After the Bologna reforms in 2005 the relevant degree is Master of Law. The lower, bachelor level law degree is *oikeusnotaari*; notary of law. The Finnish universities offer also a Master in International and Comparative Law, which does not qualify for the legal profession in Finland. Recognition of law degrees in other EU and other ETA countries requires a complementary exam at a Finnish law faculty. See Act on Recognition of Professional Qualifications (*Laki ammattipätevyyden tunnustamisesta* 1093/2007) and http://www.oph.fi/english/services/recognition/national_contact_point_for_the_professional_qualifications_directive.

majority of the population in the jurisdiction, that is, either in Finnish or in Swedish. In addition, the judge must have satisfactory qualifications in the other official language of the country.[4]

75. The judge must have shown, through his experience, a good knowledge (*perehtyneisyys*) in the responsibilities of the position. The one-year traineeship (clerkship) in the district court is no longer a formal requirement, but it is still a popular way of gaining experience for young lawyers, leading to the title of vice-judge (trained on the bench). Besides training in the district court, the traineeship can include a six month period in the appeal court or in the administrative court (District Court Act § 14).

76. In addition, the judge to be must have the appropriate personal qualifications for the office. In particular, the judge must be just and fair-minded. In order to be appointed in the position of a chief judge in any court, one must have the capacity to lead. There are special provisions on expert members, such as land court surveyors, of the court (District Court Act § 13a).

77. In the case of Supreme Court justices, special emphasis is put on their legal qualification, since they must have excellent knowledge of the law.

78. Specific disqualifications that are related to an individual case are regulated in Chapter 13 of the Code of Procedure, which was reformed in 2001 (Part V, Chapter 1, § 1).

B. Lay Judges

79. In district courts, lay judges participate in the adjudication of criminal law cases and in land court matters (Real Estate Formation Act *Kiinteistönmuodostamislaki* 554/1995 § 243; 1180/2000). Finnish citizens who live in the jurisdiction of the court qualify as lay judges. They have to be non-bankrupt and their civil competence may not have been restricted. The lay judges must be over 25 years of age and they cannot be appointed after their 65th birthday (District Court Act § 6).

80. Persons who work close to the judiciary do not qualify for lay judges. Such professions are employees in ordinary courts, in penal institutions and in enforcement authorities, customs officers, prosecutors, advocates, the police and other personnel, who carry out criminal investigation (District Court Act § 6.2). The disqualification of a lay judge in a criminal case has been subject to adjudication in KKO:2008:95.

4. The Act on Judicial Appointments § 12 (as amended by Law 592/2009) and the District Court Act § 1b (as amended by Law 1751/2009). The judges are required to register any commitments or secondary occupations. A law to this effect has been enacted but it has not become into force yet (*Laki tuomareiden sidonnaisuus- ja sivutoimirekisteristä 565/2015)*.

II. End of Functions

81. A tenured judge is in principle irremovable. According to the Constitution § 103.1 a judge can only be removed by a decision of a court.

82. The age of retirement is 68, which applies also to lay judges (Civil Servants Act § 35 as amended by Law (685/2004) and District Court Act § 6). According to legislation on civil servants a judge is obliged to resign if he has become unable to serve in the office due to (permanent) illness or disability. Under such circumstances, a judge can also be removed by a decision of the court (Civil Servants Act; *Valtion virkamieslaki* 750/1994 § 46).

III. Discipline

83. The ultimate sanction for offences in office is prosecution. The Constitution gives everyone a right to request punishment or liability for damages of a civil servant for an unlawful act or omission in the performance of a public function (§ 118.3). This historically grounded right includes the right to bring charges against a civil servant, including the judges. Charges that should be heard by the High Court of Impeachment are excluded from this right.

84. A special court, the High Court of Impeachment has jurisdiction over charges against members of the Supreme Court and the Supreme Administrative Court (Constitution § 101). The Court of Appeal has jurisdiction over offences in office committed by district court judges and the Supreme Court for the judges of Courts of Appeal (Court of Appeal Act § 2.2 (957/2000) and the Supreme Court Act § 1, 4).

85. The disciplinary measures of the Civil Servants Act are not applied to judges.

IV. Supervision

86. The higher courts supervise the lower courts mainly in the context of legal review (Constitution § 99.2 and Court of Appeal Act § 2.3). The Supreme Court and the Courts of Appeal have the duty to take initiative to correct any defects they detect. The courts are, however, independent in their adjudication and the higher courts cannot give the lower court orders on how to judge. Thus, the supervision is more indirect and is enforced through precedents and general discussions about the development of legal processes, administration, etc.

87. Both the Chancellor of Justice and the Parliamentary Ombudsman supervise the courts (Constitution §§ 106–107). An important part of their activities is based on the petitions from the members of the public who feel that their rights have been violated in the use of public power, including the courts. The Chancellor of Justice and the Ombudsman cannot change the decisions of the authorities, even less those of the courts, but they have the power to bring charges against the civil servants and to give a reminder for improper conduct or application of law. They can also seek extraordinary review of a decision. In recent years, the ombudsman has taken a role in the supervision of the civil servants by giving opinions on the correct procedure or interpretation of the law. In the supervision of the courts the role of the chancellor and the Ombudsman is limited because their supervision is subsidiary in relation to the ordinary means of review.

Chapter 2. The Bar

§1. Exercise of the Legal Profession

88. Traditionally the trial in the district courts has been informal in such a way that the parties should have been able to proceed by themselves, without an attorney. Many district court judges understood that their role was to adjust the proceedings to the possibilities of the 'common man' to proceed by himself. As the society and the law have become more complicated, this ideal has become more difficult to sustain. Especially the reforms of the process in the 1990s have made the use of an attorney almost a necessity. In principle, the parties still have a right to process themselves, that is, without an attorney in all courts, up to the Supreme Court. However, a plead for the extraordinary review in the Supreme Court must be made by an attorney (OK 15:1.4; 718/2011)

89. The party has a right to be represented by an attorney in a civil case, unless the court orders that the party must be present in person at a hearing. Of course, the party always has a right to be accompanied and assisted by an attorney.

90. The competence to represent a party in a court is given to members of the bar (see §2 below), public legal aid attorneys (§3 below) and lawyers who have obtained a license (paragraph 90 below). Exceptions to this rule are: summary proceedings, non-contested application matters, registration matters and land cases, in which persons without a law degree may act as counsellors (OK 15:2.4). An employee and a civil servant, who have a Master degree in law, can represent their employer in a matter that belongs to their duties (OK 15:2.2-3). In a labour law matter, a lawyer employed by a trade union or an association of the employers (OK 15:2.2) can act as a legal counsel and representative. In debt adjustment for private persons, a professional debt counsellor may act as a representative of the debtor. Certain restrictions to representation apply to members of the judiciary and their family (OK 15:3).

91. Persons with a qualification to act as advocates in another EU Member State may also act as legal counsels in Finland (OK 15:2.2; 764/2001).

92. Since 2013, legal representation in the court requires a license. The license is given by a Board for Licensed Legal Counsels. The board consists of three judges, one licensed counsel and one representative of the legal education. The licensed counsels are under the supervision of the Bar Association, the Board for licensed counsels and the Chancellor of Justice. The Disciplinary Board of the Bar Association can impose the sanctions on a licensed counsel as on a member of the Bar. The license can be revoked and a pecuniary sanction can be imposed only by the Board for Licensed Counsels (See Act on Licensed Counsels *Laki luvan saaneista oikeudenkäyntiavustajista* 715/2011).

93. The qualification for a licensed counsel is a Master's level degree in law that qualifies for the legal profession in Finland, knowledge and familiarity with the duties of a counsel, honesty and suitability for the profession, who is not bankrupt or under guardianship. The knowledge and familiarity with the duties of a counsel can be proven by passing the bar exam, by having completed the court traineeship, by working for at least one year as a prosecutor or by working at least for one year in other task learning the duties of a counsel (Act on Licensed Counsels § 2).

94. The attorney has to present a proxy or a power of attorney, which traditionally is written and which gives the counsels general, 'open' right to representation. If the attorney accompanies the client to the court, the proxy is given orally. Advocates and public legal aid attorneys are relieved of the obligation to present a proxy, unless the court specifically orders it. In an electronic summons application reference to a proxy is sufficient. The court may order the attorney to present the proxy if necessary (OK 15:4; 259/2002). The tradition of 'open' proxies made flexible substitution of an advocate possible. The advocate is allowed to rely on a colleague if he is temporarily restrained from appearing in the case.

§2. The Bar Association

I. Conditions for Admission

95. The title 'advocate' is reserved for the use by members of the Finnish Bar Association which is a public and legally regulated association (Advocates Act). The Ministry of Justice approves the Statute of the Bar Association (Advocates Act § 2.3; Ministry of Justice Decision on the Approval of the Finnish Bar Association By-Laws 540/2012). Today the association has 2100 members (http://www.asianajajaliitto.fi/asianajajaliitto/liitto_lyhyesti).

96. The membership is subject to specific qualifications. The members are obligated to follow the rules and the Code of Conduct of the Bar Association and they are under the supervision of the Association and its council.

97. The executive board of the Bar Association makes the decisions on membership. To be accepted as a member and, thus, to have the right to use the title of advocate one has to be at least 25 years of age and a citizen of Finland or any other country in the European Economic Area (EEA). In addition, one may not be a bankrupt and must have full legal capacity, the same academic degree in law as is required of a judge (Master; see Part I Chapter 1, I A above), the necessary professional skills and working experience and a suitable personal character and way of life (the Advocates Act § 3).

98. The professional skills referred to above, besides the academic degree, are tested through an examination arranged by the Association. The examination focuses on the legal and ethical duties and responsibilities of the advocate.

99. The required working experience consists of four years in legal responsibilities, of which at least two years have to be in an advocate's office or similar tasks.

If the applicant has qualifications of an advocate in another State in the EEA, he may acquire the academic qualification through a special examination arranged by the University of Helsinki. Alternatively, an advocate from another Member State of the EU may qualify after three years of practice in Finland (The Finnish Bar Association By-Laws § 5).

100. Civil servants do not qualify as advocates, with the exception of public legal aid attorneys who may apply for the title or who may choose not to do so. Since the title is highly respected, many public legal aid attorneys have obtained it (the Advocates Act § 3.4; see Rosti et al. 2008).

II. Rights and Duties

101. The advocate's duties and responsibilities are defined in the Code of Procedure, in the Advocates Act and, most importantly, in the Code of Conduct, confirmed by the general assembly of the Bar Association (Rules of proper professional conduct for advocates (1.9.2009 http://www.asianajajaliitto.fi/files/1044/B_01_Code_of_conduct_for_lawyers_%2815.1.2009%29.pdf).

102. The role of the advocate is to protect the rights of the client and, thus, the advocate's first and foremost duty is to be loyal to the client. As the client's interests are sometimes, and in criminal matters most of the time, opposite to those of the State, independence is one of the key notions in organizing the advocate's profession. The Advocates Act and the Code of Conduct include concrete regulations on, for example, how secrecy, confidentiality, economic liability and independence from conflicts of interest are guaranteed. It must be remembered, however, that the advocate also has responsibilities towards the courts, other authorities and even the opposite party. By following the rules of professional and ethical conduct, the independence of the profession is guaranteed in the long run.

103. The advocate can run his practice in a company with another advocate. An advocate can practice in the form of a company with limited liability or in partnership with another professional but an advocate only if the Board of the Bar Association grants a permit to do so. Even then, the partner is personally liable for the advocate's tasks he undertakes (The Advocates Act § 5.2).

III. Discipline

104. The supervision and control of advocates is the responsibility of the Bar Association. This arrangement is seen as the utmost guarantee of the independence of the profession. In addition, the Chancellor of Justice and the courts have certain supervisory functions.

105. The board of the Bar Association has the responsibility for the supervision, even though the Association's Disciplinary Board handles most of the individual complaints it receives. The Association has a right to request information from the advocate and to impose control(s) on his conduct. The disciplinary penalties the Association can impose are reprimand, caution, monetary penalty and disbarment from the membership. The monetary penalty, between EUR 500 and 15 000, payable to the Bar Association was added to the law in 2004 (The Advocates Act § 7.5 and 10 (697/2004)). The Chancellor of Justice and the advocate have the right to appeal the decisions of the Disciplinary Board and the board of the Association to the Appeal Court of Helsinki in disciplinary matters (Advocates Act § 10).

§3. Public Attorneys

106. State funded public legal aid offices cover the whole country and give legal aid in criminal and civil matters. Since 2002, when the legal aid was transferred from the communities to the State, the attorneys work as civil servants of the state (Legal Aid Act *Oikeusapulaki* 257/2002).

107. In court proceedings, a party with scarce financial resources can either choose a public legal aid attorney or turn to a private attorney who then requests a decision on legal aid and appointment as a private legal aid attorney from the legal aid office. (Legal Aid Act § 8, see Part VI Chapter 2; Rosti et al. 2008).

Chapter 3. The Bailiffs

§1. Exercise of the Profession

I. The Writ Servers

108. The writ servers (bailiffs) are civil servants of the courts.

II. The Enforcement Authorities

109. The enforcement of judgments is organized in regional enforcement authorities, which are State authorities. There are twenty-two enforcement authorities at the moment. The head of the enforcement authority is the execution officer and the assistant execution officers (bailiffs), who are State civil servants, carry out the practical work (see further Part IX, Chapter 2, § 1).

§2. Public Institutions and Private Organizations

110. As explained, state civil servants carry out the functions of the bailiff. Private persons can also serve the summons. However, there are no professional writ servers in the private sector. The function of debt collection is practiced by several private debt collection agencies but their powers are limited when compared to those of enforcement authorities.

Part II. Jurisdiction

Chapter 1. Domestic Jurisdiction

§1. Subject Matter Jurisdiction

I. Factors to be Taken into Account

111. The basic rule is that the general courts have jurisdiction over all civil disputes. If there is no specific rule that allocates the matter to any other court, board or body, then the general courts have jurisdiction in the case. Special courts that have been given jurisdiction in certain matters that otherwise would belong to the general courts have already been described in Part I, Chapter 1, § 1 *supra.*

112. The first instance for civil suits is a district court. The appeal courts have no competence to act as first instance in civil cases. Only certain matters in international family law, such as a request of returning an abducted child to the country of origin are handled by the appeal court as a first instance (Child Custody Act § 5:31; 186/1994). The matters in which the certain district courts have been given special jurisdiction are explained in section III *infra.*

113. The rules on subject matter jurisdiction are generally obligatory and the parties cannot dispose of the jurisdiction. However, as will be discussed in Part X, the parties may agree that the arbitrators handle a dispute. Such an agreement is dispositive also in the meaning that if one party takes the case to a district court and the defendant does not invoke the arbitration agreement, the district court has jurisdiction over the case.

II. Main Claims and Ancillary Claims

114. The basic rule is that the court must have competence over all claims including the counter claims and set-off. A specific rule governing the jurisdiction of the Market Court in intellectual property rights and connected claims is found in the Act on Proceedings in Market Court (*Laki oikeudenkäynnistä markkinaoikeudessa* 100/2013) § 5, channelling these claims to Market Court.

III. Overview of the Jurisdiction of the Different Courts

A. *Special Courts*

115. The Labour Court has jurisdiction over disputes concerning the validity, interpretation and the breach of collective agreements (Act on the Labour Court *Laki työtuomioistuimesta* 646/1974). Both collective agreements between the organizations of employees and employers and collective agreements in the public sector belong to the jurisdiction of the Labour Court. The Labour Court handles about 100 cases every year. The verdict of the Labour Court is final, with no right to appeal.

116. The parties in the Labour Court are, as a rule, the parties to the collective agreement (Act on the Labour Court § 12). Disputes between an individual employee and employer are handled by the district courts unless they involve the interpretation of a collective agreement.

117. The Labour Court is based on a tripartite principle. The judges are nominated after the proposal of the parties in the labour market, representing equally the employers, the employees and the civil servants. The chief judge, his deputy and two judges are impartial and have the qualification for a judgeship. Only the chief judge and his deputy serve full time, other judges are part time. The quorum is six judges, two of whom represent the employees, alternatively the civil servants when the dispute concerns a collective agreement of the public sector, two the employers and two are impartial (Act on the Labour Court §§ 2–8. Generally about Labour Court, see www.oikeus.fi/tyotuomioistuin/2024.htm).

118. The Market Court has jurisdiction over a number of issues concerning market law as has been specified in the law on market court and the law on jurisdiction in market matters. These include issues in competition law, public procurement, marketing and consumer contracts, unfair conditions in business contracts, etc. In the reform of 2013 jurisdiction over matters in intellectual property rights were transferred from the Helsinki district court to the Market Court (Act on the Market Court *Laki markkinaoikeudesta* 99/2013 and Act on Proceedings in Market Court).

B. *Boards*

119. Several boards have been established to give opinions or binding decisions on matters that fall within their jurisdiction. Boards that have been vested with the power to give binding decisions are especially found in fields that fall between public and private law regulation. Especially, the employers are legally obliged to insure their workers and, consequently, the insurance is regulated by law, but the insurance companies are private commercial companies. The decisions of insurance companies can be appealed to the Accident Insurance Appeals Board (The Employment Accidents Act § 53; The Worker's Pension Act *Työntekijän eläkelaki* 395/2006 § 128). The decisions of Accident Insurance Appeals Board are binding with a possibility to appeal to the Insurance Court. In a similar manner, the decisions of pension companies can be appealed to the Pension Board with a further appeal to the Insurance Court. The decisions of the Insurance Court can be appealed to the Supreme Court.

120. Also, in matters of safety in the working environment a special board, the Labour Council, may give exceptions from the legal requirements of the law (Act on the Labour Council and Derogation Permits Concerning Labour Protection *Laki työneuvostosta ja eräistä työsuojelun poikkeusluvista* 400/2004).

121. The Finnish collective agreements, which are generally applied in the branch, set out the minimum conditions of all employment relations in the relevant branch. The difficulty has been to identify which collective agreements have such a general applicability. After 2001, a special board, the Confirmation Commission, has been set up to confirm general applicability (Act on Confirmation of the General Applicability of Collective Agreements *Laki työehtosopimuksen yleissitovuuden vahvistamisesta* 56/2001, especially § 9).

122. The Consumer Disputes Board is the most important of the boards that only give opinions that are not binding (Act on the Consumer Disputes Board *Laki kuluttajariitalautakunnasta* 8/2007).

123. One general advantage of the boards for the consumers or employees is that they do not, as a main rule, have the risk that they are obliged to pay the costs of litigation if they lose the case.

C. Special Jurisdiction for District Courts

124. Generally, all district courts and appeal courts have the jurisdiction in all civil cases. However, certain district courts are given jurisdiction in certain matters that require special expertise. Special functional jurisdiction is given to certain district courts in land cases, corporate reorganization cases and maritime cases.

125. Class actions in consumer law cases are allocated to six district courts (Act on Class Actions *Ryhmäkannelaki* 444/2007 § 3).

126. In maritime cases, seven district courts serve as maritime courts and their jurisdictions cover the whole country. Also, in these cases the court has a possibility to get the assistance of two experts who do not belong to the decision-making bench (Maritime Law *Merilaki* 674/1994 Ch. 21 as amended by 1754/2008).

127. The jurisdiction in land cases, that is, in disputes relating to the formation of land estates, etc., is also assigned to eight district courts (Real Estate Formation Act § 241a).

128. Reorganization of corporations and other businesses is assigned to fourteen district courts. The appeals of the decisions of the enforcement authority are assigned to fourteen courts (Restructuring of Enterprises Act *Laki yrityksen saneerauksesta* 47/1993 § 67 as amended by 1754/2008; Enforcement Code *Ulosottokaari* 705/2007 11:2 as amended by 1756/2009).

§2. VENUE (TERRITORIAL JURISDICTION)

I. Factors to be Taken into Account

129. Chapter 10 of the Code of Procedure regulating the venue has been reformed in 2009. The purpose of the reform was to modernize the rules on jurisdiction, to concentrate the most important rules to the Code of Procedure from special laws and to increase the rights of the parties to agree upon jurisdiction, unless it is necessary to protect the weaker party through mandatory jurisdiction rules, and to make the regulation more flexible. The main principles of jurisdiction, however, remained the same (HE 70/2008).

The rules on venue in civil procedure are mostly dispositive. If the rule is dispositive, the parties can agree on another venue (OK 10:19). Even if there is no prior agreement on the venue, the defendant can respond in another venue. If the defendant does not make an objection when she first responds in the case, the court will be competent to hear the case (OK 10:21). If the defendant remains passive, that is, does not respond to the charge or does not come to the first hearing, the court shall dismiss the case. The venue is determined on the basis of the situational facts when the suit is filed. If the basis for the venue changes, the court remains competent (OK 10:20).

130. For several civil actions the law stipulates a forum, which is related to the nature of the claim and which is alternative with the general *forum domicilii.* Some rules on venue are mandatory, such as *forum hereditatis*, and the court must observe such a venue ex officio. Even after the reform, special provisions on jurisdiction in other legislation supersede the rules of Chapter 10 (HE 70/2009, 18). Examples of such rules in domestic law are Road Transport Act (*Tiekuljetussopimuslaki* 345/1979) § 42.2 and Act on Equality between Women and Men (*Laki naisten ja miesten välisestä tasa-arvosta* 609/1986) § 12.

II. Main Claims and Ancillary Claims

131. The rules on joint action in Chapter 18 of the Code of Procedure give the possibility to combine several actions to be handled in one trial. Correspondingly, OK 10:10 gives the court jurisdiction over such joint actions (*forum connexitatis*). If several persons are defendants in the same lawsuit, the case can be heard where the court has venue for one of the defendants (OK 10:10,2–3). Also, a counteraction can be heard in the same court as the original action (*forum connexitatis* OK 10:10,3). The jurisdiction cannot be based on the rules of *forum connexitatis* if one of the actions should be processed in another venue on the basis of a mandatory rule on jurisdiction. *Forum connexitatis* cannot be based on an agreement on the venue against a defendant who is not party to the agreement.

III. Overview of the Different Rules

132. The court of the defendant's domicile has a general territorial competence in civil suits against the defendant (*forum domicilii*) according to OK 10:1. It is called the defendant's general forum or general jurisdiction. The defendant's domicile is the place where she resides permanently or that is registered as her domicile in the general population register. A registered company, an association, a trust, a municipality or other private or public body has a *forum domicilii* where it has its registered domicile or where its main quarters of administration are located (Limited Liability Companies Act *Osakeyhtiölaki* 624/2006 24:1 as amended by Law 1752/2009). A suit against the State can be filed in the court in the place where the authority that represents the State in the matter is located (OK 10:2). Alternatively, a suit against the State may be filed in the general forum of the claimant (OK 10:4).

133. The following venues are alternatives to the *forum domicilii*. In disputes over a transaction that has been made in the operation of a business branch or other establishment, the defendant may be sued in the place of that establishment *forum negotii* (OK 10:3). A consumer may file a suit against an entrepreneur in the court where the consumer has his domicile (OK 10:5). In disputes over an employment contract, a suit can be brought where the work is normally done or, if the work is not customarily performed in one jurisdiction, where the employer has his establishment (OK 10:6). Claims to compensation on the basis of a crime are usually processed in the criminal proceedings. Claims to compensation as civil actions can be brought in *forum delicti*, that is, where the damage was caused or the negligent action should have been performed (OK 10:7). The claimant may bring a tort action in his *forum domicile* when it is based on the Traffic Insurance Act (*Liikennevakuutuslaki* 279/1959), the Patient Injury Act, the Product Liability Act (*Tuotevastuulaki* 694/1990), the Environmental Damage Insurance Act (*Laki ympäristövahinkovakuutuksesta* 81/1998) or the Rail Traffic Liability Act (*Raideliikennevastuulaki* 113/1999).

134. The disputes over immovable property can be adjudicated in *forum rei sitae*. After the reform of 2009, *forum rei sitae* is dispositive and alternative to the *forum domicilii* of the defendant (OK 10:8). Disputes over immovable property include disputes related to ownership, mortgage, lease, other right to use, tort, recovery of sale-price or rent. Finally, alimony claims can be adjudicated both in *forum domicilii* of the defendant, claimant and the beneficiary (OK 10:9).

135. Some venues are mandatory. After the 2009 reform, the number of mandatory venues has decreased. Still, jurisdiction in family law matters is mostly indispositive. An application for divorce or division of matrimonial property after divorce can be filed in the court where one of the spouses has domicile (OK 10:11).

A claim for the custody of children or visitation rights is processed where the child or the defendant has domicile (OK 10:14). It can also be adjudicated together with the divorce in the venue of divorce case (Child Custody Act § 13. See also Act on the Maintenance of a Child *Laki lapsen elatuksesta* 704/1975 § 13 and Marriage Act *Avioliittolaki* 234/1929 § 31).

136. Disputes over the estate of a deceased person are handled in the court in the place where the deceased person had his domicile (OK 10:17). This forum is also mandatory. A subsidiary forum, if the forum of the OK 10:17 is not available, is where the estate is located (OK 10:18.1 point 9).

137. If no court has jurisdiction over the case, secondary rules of jurisdiction in OK 10:18 can be applied. Thus, if the defendant has no domicile, the suit can be brought where she resides or she has had a domicile. A pecuniary claim or claim over ownership can be brought in jurisdiction where the defendant has property. Divorce and division of matrimonial property can be brought where one of the spouses last had domicile. Also other family disputes can be brought in the last place of domicile (see OK 10:18.1 points 4–7). If none of these rules applies, the District Court of Helsinki has jurisdiction.

§3. Resolution of Jurisdiction Conflicts

138. Each court has competence over its own jurisdiction. If the rule on jurisdiction is dispositive, the defendant has to make an objection before the defendant responds in the subject matter (OK 10:21;16:1). If the court finds that it has no jurisdiction over the case, it shall transfer the case to the correct court. If the competent court cannot be identified without difficulty, the court does not need to do that (OK 10:22). The plaintiff can then file the case in another court. The decisions on jurisdiction can be appealed either separately or together with the decision on the main matter (OK 16:3).

139. The Supreme Court has the final competence in conflicts over jurisdiction. According to the Supreme Court Act § 2, point 5, the Supreme Court has the competence to decide whether a general court, special court or an administrative body has jurisdiction over a case.

140. If the higher court, handling an appeal, finds that a lower court does not have jurisdiction over the matter, it may transfer the case to the correct venue (OK 10:24.1). The case is not transferred if all the parties oppose it. The Supreme Court has final competence over conflicts over jurisdiction between the courts. If two (or more) courts hold by final decisions that none of them has jurisdiction over the case, a party can petition the Supreme Court that decides what court is the right venue and refers the case to that court (OK 10:24.2).

Chapter 2. International Jurisdiction

§1. Rules Applicable in the Absence of a Treaty

141. The reform of 2009 introduced rules on international jurisdiction into Finnish law. Today, important rules on international jurisdiction are found in binding international documents, especially in EU law. Thus, the new rules in OK 10:25–26 are subsidiary to these international rules. It has to be noted that the new rules on international jurisdiction have been modelled in congruence with the principles of the EU instruments on jurisdiction.

142. The basic principle of international jurisdiction in OK 10 is that when a case has a strong connection to Finland, the Finnish courts have jurisdiction. And to the contrary, jurisdiction should not be based on a weak connection to Finland (no extra-orbitant jurisdiction). Generally, the jurisdiction as regulated in Chapter 10 of the Code of Procedure indicates that the case has a connection to Finland and the Finnish courts have jurisdiction over the case. The court may find, however, that there is no basis for jurisdiction if a judgment by a Finnish court in the case could clearly not have legal relevance for the parties (OK 10:25.2 p 1).

143. In special cases, the Finnish courts have jurisdiction even if the connection to Finland is somewhat weaker. This is the case if a consumer has *forum domicilii* in Finland or the case can be combined with another case (*forum connexitatis*). The international jurisdiction may then be decided on the basis of convenience. The factors taken into account are the presentation of the evidence, the costs to the parties and other circumstances. However, if the procedure to be followed or the legislation to be applied in the court of a foreign state would be contrary to the public policy in Finland, the Finnish court has jurisdiction. In still relevant case law, KKO:2007:68, the connection to Finland through *forum connexitatis* was held to be too weak to create jurisdiction.

144. Jurisdiction may sometimes be based on the connection recognized in the rules of secondary jurisdiction or on other essential circumstance (OK 10:25.2). Examples of such situations might be that a contractual obligation should be performed in Finland or that the defendant has agreed not to engage in a certain activity in Finland (HE 70/2009, 50). Also in such situations, the international jurisdiction may then be decided on the basis of convenience. The factors taken into account are the presentation of the evidence, the costs to the parties and other circumstances. However, if the procedure to be followed or the legislation to be applied in the court of a foreign state would be contrary to the public policy in Finland, the Finnish court has jurisdiction (OK 10:25.3).

145. International jurisdiction of the Finnish courts in divorce cases is regulated in Marriage Act § 119. If one of the spouses has domicile in Finland or if one of the spouses has had domicile or other close connection to Finland and the divorce cannot reasonably be processed where one of the spouses lives, then Finnish courts have jurisdiction. Divorce, if neither spouse is domiciled in Finland, can be filed in the District Court of Helsinki. International jurisdiction in other matters related to marriage and divorce is regulated in the Marriage Act §§ 126–127. International jurisdiction concerning family law is also regulated, for example, in the Adoption Act (*Adoptiolaki* 22/2012) § 65 and the Child Custody Act §§ 19–20.

§2. International Treaties and European Law

146. International jurisdiction in the Member States of the EU is governed by Council Regulation 1215/2015 on jurisdiction and the recognition and enforcement of judgments in civil and commercial matters (Brussels I Regulation). Jurisdiction in European payment orders and European small claims procedure belongs to the District Court of Helsinki (Laws 753/2008 and 754/2008 § 2).

147. In family matters, the jurisdiction is governed by Council Regulation 2201/2003 concerning jurisdiction and the recognition and enforcement of judgments in matrimonial matters and the matters of parental responsibility (Brussels II Regulation). In inheritance matters the jurisdiction and enforcement are governed by Regulation 650/2012 on jurisdiction, applicable law, recognition and enforcement of decisions and acceptance and enforcement of authentic instruments in matters of succession and on the creation of a European Certificate of Succession.

148. There are special laws that contain a few clauses on international jurisdiction in matters governed by these laws. Such provisions are usually based on an international treaty. An example of such a jurisdiction clause is the Act on Road Transfers (*Tiekuljetussopimuslaki* 345/1979) § 42.

Part III. Actions and Claims

Chapter 1. Actions

§1. Definitions

I. Actions by Summons

149. A civil trial can be instigated either by *summons (haaste)* or *application (hakemus)*. Summons is the ordinary form of starting a proceeding and it is used in all cases except in those that are started by application according to the OK, Chapter 8. Summons is used in monetary claims, contract and commercial disputes, and most other civil matters of dispositive character.

150. The content of the application for the summons is regulated in detail in OK 5:1. The application shall include the specified claim by the plaintiff and the grounds, on which the claim is based. The plaintiff shall indicate what evidence the plaintiff will present and what he will prove with each piece of evidence. Thus, the plaintiff should at least give the evidentiary theme of each piece of evidence. Furthermore, the plaintiff should note a claim for the compensation of legal costs and, if necessary, a note on the jurisdiction of the court.

151. In addition, the application for a summons includes technical information about the names, occupations and domiciles of the parties, their attorneys and the witnesses, and other persons to be heard and their contact information.

152. Summary actions (summaarinen asia) for payment claims are also instigated by summons in district courts. Summary actions are allowed for monetary claims of a specified amount, for claims for repossession of property and for eviction. Specific rules govern the summons in summary claims (OK 5.3), allowing for a simplified form. Since the basis for the claim is usually based on a written document, no additional evidence is required. If it is known that the defendant will dispute the claim, summary form is not allowed. In practice, however, the claimant's statement that the payment is not disputed is sufficient.

II. Actions by Application

153. Application as a form of action was first regulated in 1987 by the Law on application proceedings (*Laki hakemusasioiden käsittelystä yleisessä alioikeudessa* 307/1986). Application was designed as a less formal and complicated form of proceedings used in other court matters than civil and criminal actions. After the reforms of procedural law in the 1990s, the differences between application matters and ordinary proceedings have diminished. The regulation of applications was transferred to Chapter 8 ('Procedure in Application Matters') of the Code of Procedure in 2002 (768/2002).

154. Also, matters that the court takes up on its own initiative or after a notification are processed according to the rules of Chapter 8 of the Code of Procedure.

155. There is no general rule defining what matters should be filed as application matters. Instead, a number of rules in material legislation state that a matter should be filed in the court by an application. Traditionally, the registration of certain documents, for example of prenuptial agreements, was an application matter (*jurisdictio voluntaria*). These registration matters were recently removed from the district courts to other authorities. Still valid examples of *jurisdictio voluntaria* are the nomination of a trustee according to inheritance law or of a guardian, which are handled as an application matter (Code of Inheritance *Perintökaari* 40/1965; 19:12a; Guardianship Services Act *Laki holhoustoimesta* 442/1999 § 69).

156. During the 1980s and 1990s, new groups of cases were defined as application matters. Most importantly, most matters concerning family law, such as, divorce, end of marital cohabitation and adoption are application matters. Insolvency proceedings are likewise instigated by application. As an example of application matters, a request to a publisher, a broadcaster or a server to stop the distribution of a published network message is handled according to the application procedure of OK Chapter 8.[5]

157. Unlike in ordinary proceedings, in application matters the parties are not necessarily in dispute when the application is made. As new groups of cases fall under Chapter 8 of the Code of Procedure, these matters have become more contentious. Therefore, also proceedings in application matters and in ordinary civil cases have come more alike.

158. Chapter 8 gives the court a flexible framework for the procedure. Simple, non-contentious applications can be handled quickly in a written procedure. In a disputed case, a hearing is arranged if a party demands a hearing or if the court deems a hearing necessary for the clarification of the case. In a disputed case the court can

5. Marriage Act § 28 (411/1987); Act on Child Custody and Right of Access § 14; Adoption Act § 51.2; Bankruptcy Act (*Konkurssilaki* 120/2004) 7:4; Act on the Adjustment of the Debts of a Private Individual §§ 49–50; Restructuring of Enterprises Act §§ 68–69; Freedom of Expression Act § 18 (463/2011).

decide that the rules of ordinary civil procedure are followed (OK 8:4). Such a decision is mandatory in contested family law cases.

159. The rules in Chapter 8 are not exhaustive. When material legislation contains specific rules on procedure, these supervene the rules of Chapter 8. For example, Chapter 7 of the Bankruptcy Act of 2004 as well as other insolvency laws contain several important rules on procedure. The other chapters of the Code of Procedure, regulating ordinary civil procedure, are subsidiary to Chapter 8 and they are followed when a procedural issue is not regulated in Chapter 8.

III. Class Actions

160. The Act on Class Actions came into force in 1 October 2007. According to it, the Consumer Ombudsman may bring a class action in the six designated district courts against an enterprise on a matter that falls within her competence. Before issuing a summons, the court informs the parties of commencement of the case. After that, the plaintiff has to give all class members a possibility to join the action either by a personal letter, an email or an announcement in the newspapers. The plaintiff is obliged to prepare a supplement to the application with the names and claims of all class applicants. After that, the summons is served to the defendant. The list of class members as applicants may be amended and restricted during the preparation of the trial. A judgment in the case shall be binding on the class members who are mentioned in the judgment. The plaintiff, that is, the Consumer Ombudsman is liable to pay the costs of the defendant if she loses the case (Ervo, 2009).

§2. Admissibility

161. The doctrine of admissibility or preconditions for action *(prosessinedellytykset)* is classified in four groups:

(1) jurisdiction (see Part II);
(2) preconditions concerning the parties and their representation;
(3) rules on the filing procedure of the action; and
(4) the actionability of the claim. The most important preconditions in this group are the doctrines of res judicata and lis pendens. Also, claims that are not actionable in a court at all can be included in this group.

162. Generally, the right of action as to the proper party (2) is in accordance with the substantive law: the rights' holder has the right of action. Children below 18 years of age are represented by their parent(s) in dispositive disputes over property and civil rights. Children who are 15 but not 18 years of age have the right to dispose over their working income. In personal matters, a child who is 15 but not 18 years old has the right of action besides her custodian (OK 12:1). In KKO:1996:147 a parent/custodian was granted a right of action on behalf of under-age children in a dispute over property rights. In KKO:1992:186 such a right was denied when a father had brought charges claiming that the right to ownership belonged to his adult daughter. If a person for other reasons, such as disability or illness, does not have legal capacity, the court may appoint that person a guardian for the proceedings (OK 12:4a (560/2007)). The court may act on its own initiative (About hearing the disabled person, see KKO:2009:68; KKO:2012:109).

163. The lack of preconditions for an action may be either non-reparable or reparable. For example, lack of jurisdiction has traditionally been non-reparable; the action was dismissed and it was the responsibility of the plaintiff to refile the case in the correct forum. Today, however, the court may transfer the case to the correct venue under certain conditions. A problem in the filing procedure, usually in the service of the summons, is often reparable. A mistake in the service can often be corrected by servicing the summons anew, if the claim is not prescribed.

164. Most of the conditions for admissibility are indispositive, that is, the court has to observe them notwithstanding a statement by the defendant. Many rules on jurisdiction, however, are dispositive. The court does not observe them unless the defendant invokes such a defence already when the defendant first replies to the summons (OK 16:1; OK 10:11.2).

§3. Vexatious Litigation

165. The Code of Procedure gives several means to counteract vexatious litigation. First, the court may dismiss an action that is manifestly unfounded without even giving the summons (OK 5:6.2; see Part III Chapter 3 § Formal requirements). Second, the rules for compensation of legal costs give the court a possibility to compensate the other party for the costs of vexatious litigation. Third, the preclusion rules effectively inhibit purposeful slow-downs of the process by excluding the presentation of precluded material in the process (Part III, Chapter 2, § 2). Fourth, in some cases vexatious litigation can be labelled as criminal conduct.

166. The rules for compensation of legal costs give the court discretion to compensate the opposing party for the costs that the other party has caused by deliberate or negligent actions or omissions. First, if a party has either initiated a trial, when the opposing party has given no cause, or otherwise caused a frivolous trial on purpose or by neglect, the court may order compensation for such costs (OK 21:4). Thus, even if the party wins the trial, it may be liable for the costs of a frivolous trial. Second, if a party failed to appear in court, failed to follow the orders of the court, made a claim that he knew to be unfounded or otherwise prolonged the trial with unjustified conduct and, thus, deliberately or by negligence, caused costs to the other party, the party is liable to compensate for the incurred costs notwithstanding the outcome of the trial (OK 21:5). Besides the party, the representative or attorney of the party can be held jointly liable for the compensation of the costs so incurred (OK 21:6).

167. Chapter 29 of the Code of Procedure, including penalties for vexatious litigation, has been repealed (Law 244/2006, effective 1 October 2006). This chapter of the Code had not been reformed since 1868 and it had become *desuetudo*. According to the new Article 14:7 (244/2006), the court can impose a fine of maximum EUR 1,000 to a person who disturbs the conduct of the trial either orally at a hearing or in written pleadings.

168. Some grave forms of vexatious litigation can be criminal acts. Especially, the falsification of evidence or threatening a person who is heard in the court are crimes according to the Penal Code, Chapter 15, §§ 7–9. In some circumstances, a party can commit fraud (Penal Code 36:1) by dishonest and fraudulent conduct in the trial.

Chapter 2. Claims and Defences

§1. Definition

I. Claims for Performance

169. The nature of claims and judgments in civil procedure are classified as claims of obligation or performance (*velvoite- tai suorituskanne*), declaratory claims (*vahvistuskanne*) and constitutive claims (*muotoamiskanne*).

170. Claims for performance include monetary claims, claims for ownership and possession of a property and claims for *in natura* obligations and performance. A claim for performance can carry a negative character, for instance the requirement that the defendant restrains from certain conduct (prohibition) or tolerates some conduct by the plaintiff. It is, however, not certain to what extent negative performance actions are allowed under Finnish law. It seems to be clear that an action is allowed if the defendant already violated the plaintiff's rights and the plaintiff demands the defendant to stop the violation. To some extent, a future violence might also be cause for action. In any case, the violation must be defined concretely in the verdict in order to be executed (Code of Execution 1:1). Laws on intellectual property rights regulate actions that can be filed to prohibit activities by the defendant that violate the rights of the plaintiff (for example, the Patents Act *Patenttilaki* 550/1967 § 57 (717/1995) and the Trademarks Act *Tavaramerkkilaki* 7/1964) § 38). Protection orders, ordering a person to stop harassing and threatening another person and staying away from this protected person and his/her premises, are regulated in an Act on Restraining Orders (*Laki lähestymiskiellosta* 898/1998) that falls between criminal and civil procedure. It is not clear whether the civil injunctions regulated in Code of Procedure Chapter 7 can be used to protect a person and whether a judgment ordering a person not to harass another person can be given in ordinary civil proceedings.

171. As a main rule, the claim should be mature. In any other case, the claim will be dismissed. The exceptions to the requirement of maturity are not codified in the law, but the doctrine is quite unambiguous at this point. The claims that can be approved, even if the time for performance is not due, are the following (Lappalainen, 2012, 499–500):

(a) interest on the main obligation;
(b) maintenance, compensation or annuity that is paid in periodic payments, also for future payments;
(c) a subsidiary obligation that falls due if the primary obligation is not fulfilled;
(d) counter-obligations which must be fulfilled on the condition that the main obligation is fulfilled.

172. Claims that are conditional on the non-performance of another defendant or debtor can in some cases be processed and adjudicated as conditional claims. For example, when a personal guarantor and debtor are both defendants, the claim by the guarantor against the debtor is conditional on the payment that the guarantor has to make to the creditor. When the claims are processed in the same proceedings, the obligation of the guarantor is conditional and a conditional judgment can be given (See OK 18:5 and Part III Chapter 2 § 4 about joinder). The Act on Guaranties and Third-Party Pledges (*Laki takauksesta ja vierasvelkapanttauksesta* 361/1999) § 36.2 allows the guarantor to file a suit against the main debtor before the guarantor has paid the debt. In case KKO:2009:64 the Supreme Court stated that a claim on the responsibility of a third party could not be declared inadmissible on the basis that the debtor-claimant had not paid the compensation ordered by a court to the claimant in the first trial.

173. Summary proceedings are a special form of civil procedure in which the claimant can instigate an action in a simplified format. Summary proceedings as a separate procedure for the recovery of payment obligations, either in the district courts or in the enforcement authorities, were abolished in the 1993 reform of civil procedure. After the reform, the recovery of simple payment obligations is handled by the district courts according to a simplified civil procedure (summary proceeding).

174. The claim in a summary proceeding must be either a monetary payment obligation of a specified amount; restitution of a specified object or eviction (OK 5:3).

175. The claimant must notify the court that he assumes that the claim will not be contested. The summary action is filed in a simple form; the claimant states the relevant facts of the case in the summons application and specifies the contract or other written document on which the claim is based. Since the claim is presumed to be non-contested, the claimant does not need to invoke any proof of the claim, nor attach any documents. If the claim is based on a negotiable promissory note, check or bill of exchange, the original document should be attached (OK 5:14,3). About the proceedings, see Part VIII 1.

II. Declaratory Claims

176. Declaratory actions are actions to confirm a substantial legal relationship or duty without ordering a performance (positive declaratory action) or to confirm that no such relationship exists (negative declaratory action). For example, it is possible to claim that the court confirms a breach of a patent or that a defendant is liable for compensation for a negligent action without claiming the actual payment of compensation. A declaratory action can also confirm ownership. As a negative declaratory action, it is possible to claim that the court confirms that a contract between the parties is invalid.

177. A general rule is, however, that only claims that have a concrete legal effect on the relationship between the parties are allowed. Thus, a claim for a statement from the court on an abstract question on legal interpretation is not allowed. Nor are claims for a confirmation that an empirical fact exits allowed.

178. In addition, it is required that there is uncertainty about the legal relationship that should be confirmed and that the uncertainty is to the plaintiff's detriment. The possibility of a performance claim does not preclude the plaintiff from filing a declaratory action to confirm that the legal relationship exists (Lappalainen, 2012, 501–503), which can be sensible so that the costs of litigation can be reduced.

III. Constitutive Claims

179. Constitutive actions are matters in which the judgment is necessary in order to change legal status or relationships. Constitutive actions are most common in matters concerning personal status, such as divorce, paternity, guardianship and adoption. Also, some actions concerning the law of obligations and property, such as annulment of a deed or a document, may include a constitutive element.

180. As a principle, constitutive actions are only allowed when it is mentioned in a specific provision in the law. In family law, the parties of the suit are also defined in the law. For example, the spouses have the right to action in divorce cases (and the children have no standing) and the child and the father have standing in a paternity case.[6] With the exception of paternity, these constitutive actions are filed as application matters. Typically, the constitutive judgment has res judicata effect *inter omnia*, that is, it is valid against everybody.

§2. DISTINCTIONS

I. Elements of Actions

181. The elements of an action are divided into claims, grounds and evidentiary facts. The claims, whether performance, declaratory or constitutive, must be substantiated by legal grounds. Legal grounds are the foundation of the claim and of immediate relevance for the approval of the claim. In the terminology of the Code of Procedure, the legal grounds are referred to as 'grounds' (*perusteet*) or 'circumstances' (*seikat*). Evidentiary facts may be alleged to support the grounds, but they have no immediate relevance for the approval of the claim.

182. The court is bound in its verdict by the claims and the legal grounds invoked by the parties (OK 24:3; KKO:1989:105). This burden does not cover the evidentiary facts – the court may rely on them notwithstanding who has presented

6. Nor does a child have a standing or right to file for his or her own custody; the right to file is defined in the Act on Child Custody and Right of Access § 14. Accordingly, the parents, a custodian and or the social welfare board have the right to file for a custody proceeding. The Supreme Court confirmed that the child has no right to file in KKO:2012:95.

them at the trial. Nor is the court bound by the legal characterization of the case by the parties. The principle of *jura novit curia* is understood in such a way that the court may use another legal provision in its verdict than the parties as long as the relevant grounds and the claimed outcome remain within the limits of the actions of the parties. As an example of use of another legal characterization of the matter (and not invoking new grounds), see KKO:1988:37: The plaintiff had first invoked a breach of the by-laws of the association and later to the equality of the members. This was not considered prohibited amendment of the grounds.[7]

II. Amendment of Claims

183. During the comprehensive reform of civil procedure in 1993, the regulation of amendments of claims was considered essential for the achievement of the aims of the reform, that is, for the division between the preparatory stage and the main hearing in the trial and for the realization of the principles of orality, immediacy and concentration of the main hearing. Therefore, quite a restrictive attitude towards amendments of the claims was adopted. Especially those amendments that are allowed should be presented during the preparatory stage of the trial.

184. The summons, and the claims and the legal grounds presented in it, define the object of the trial. The main principle is that the claims and the legal grounds as presented in the summons cannot be changed during the trial (OK 14:2.1 point 1). The law allows, however, important exceptions to this principle.

185. First, a claim for another performance is allowed if it is based on a circumstance that has occurred during the trial or that has become known to the plaintiff during the trial (OK 14:2.1 point 1). For example, the plaintiff has claimed compensation for the reparation of the object the plaintiff has purchased, but during the trial the plaintiff finds out that object is irreparable and claims annulment of the purchase instead. In such a case, the legal ground is allowed to be amended.

186. The law is not clear on whether 'another performance' also covers an increase in the amount of the claim. When another performance is qualitatively different and, thus, more far-reaching than the original claim, an increase in the amount of claim can also be allowed, if it is based on a new circumstance. The Supreme Court, however, in verdict KKO:2000:41, takes the position that the claimant, the victim of a crime, could not make additional claims in the appeal court on the basis of new symptoms after the district court verdict. The prohibition to change the claim in OK 14:2 is applied to a claim based on private law and presented in the criminal procedure. How far-reaching the conclusions on the interpretation of point 1 of OK

7. In KKO:2006:54 the matter was characterized as a new ground for the claim. The plaintiff (a bank) had based its claim on unjustified enrichment. Before the appellate court the bank changed its position and invoked also commitments as personal guarantors. The Supreme Court held that this was a new ground and dismissed it. The bank had explicitly not invoked the guarantor contracts before the district court, which influenced the outcome of the court's decision. However, the case shows that the borderline between legal characterization and (factual) ground is not always clear-cut.

14:2.1 are on the basis of this decision is, however, unclear. The attitude towards new or increased claims according to this point is clearly restrictive.

187. New claims are specifically mentioned in point 3 of OK 14:2,1, but the issue is relevant since amendments mentioned in point 1 of OK 14:2.1 (unlike those mentioned in point 3) are allowed in the main hearing and even in the higher courts. For example, the Supreme Court allowed a new claim on visiting rights to be presented in the Supreme Court in a suit on the parental custody of children (case KKO:1971 II 80). This is an old case and concerns an indispositive case, in which the OK 14:2 is applied but perhaps less rigorously than in dispositive cases. The case, however, illustrates a situation where the new claim can be understood as 'another performance'.

188. Second, the plaintiff may ask for a declaratory judgment on a disputed issue, which is prejudicial for the final adjudication of the matter (OK 14:2.1 point 2).

189. Third, the plaintiff may make an auxiliary claim, which is based essentially on the same ground as the original claim. Auxiliary claims are, for example, interests or legal costs (OK 14:2.1 point 3).

190. Fourth, the plaintiff may even present a new claim, if it is essentially based on the same ground as the original claim. This requirement limits the possibility to make new claims (OK 14:2.1 point 3).

191. The allowed amendments should be made during the preparation stage of the trial (OK 5:20). The district court can impose a deadline for amendments and giving notice of evidence (OK 5:22).

192. An amendment based on a change in the circumstances (OK 14:2.1 point 1) is allowed in the main trial and even in the higher courts. If the amendments mentioned in points 2 and 3 are made in the main hearing, they are dismissed if they delay the trial. The last-mentioned amendments are not allowed in the appeal court or in the Supreme Court (OK 14:2.2).

III. Amendment of Grounds

193. The prohibition against the amendment of claims does not cover a situation in which the plaintiff invokes a new legal ground to support his claim. The limit for the assertion of a new ground is that the matter is altered into another action (OK 14:2.3).

194. The interpretation of OK 14:2 paragraph 3 evolved in the doctrine from a theory of individualization towards a theory of outcome and from a restrictive attitude to a more permissive one. Today, both doctrine and practice set the claimed outcome as the criteria for non-permissible amendment of the action. As long as the claimed outcome remains the same, the plaintiff is allowed to invoke new grounds. The Supreme Court seems to have adopted this theory in its decision KKO:1990:83. The plaintiff had claimed a share of a tax on the basis of sale contract, according to which she was entitled to the return before the real estate had been sold. The plaintiff invoked as an additional ground her status as one of the heirs of the original owner. The additional ground was allowed.

195. The additional ground must be invoked during the preparation stage of the trial (OK 5:20 and 22). In the main hearing, a new ground may be allowed if the party establishes a probability that he has a valid reason for not invoking it during the preparation stage (OK 6:9). New grounds are not allowed in the higher courts unless the party establishes that he could not invoke them in the district court or that he had a valid reason for not doing so (OK 25:17 and OK 30:7). In case KKO:2003:4 the defendant employer had in the appeal court invoked a new ground for dismissal of an employee. The Supreme Court held that the defendant had not shown that it had a valid reason not to invoke the new ground in the district court and, thus, was not allowed to invoke in the appeal court either.

196. The preclusion of legal grounds in the main trial (OK 6:9) does not concern indispositive cases, in which the court has more responsibility for the clarification of the material truth.

IV. Defences

197. The defendant may present procedural and material defences. Procedural, dispositive defences must be presented when the defendant first responds to the summons. They can lead to the dismissal of the case.

198. Material defences can lead to the disapproval of the plaintiff's claim. A material defence can be based on a legal argument or on a factual ground, either a denial of the factual basis of the plaintiff's claim or a counter-fact. In addition, the defendant can present a claim for a set-off. The defendant is, in principle, allowed to change the denial or admittance of the claim more freely than the plaintiff is to amend the claim. The prohibition to amend the claim in OK 14:2 does not apply to the defendant who, in principle, can deny a claim that she has admitted earlier. It must be noted, however, that the court has the discretion to freely evaluate the evidentiary value of the withdrawal of admittance of a fact (OK 17:4).

199. The Supreme Court took rather a liberal view of allowing a new ground for denial of a claim in KKO:2010:9. In this case the plaintiff had requested that a contract condition of life-long occupancy in a sale of a half of real estate should be cancelled as the intimate partnership had ended. The district court held for the plaintiff. The defendant claimed in the appeal court that the conditions of the sale of real estate should be moderated as the outcome was unfair. The Supreme Court agreed with the defendant and submitted the case to the appeal court for reconsideration.

Two justices, however, disagreed. They found that the new claim should have been presented already in the district court.

200. The defendant is, however, bound by the preclusion rules in OK 5:20 and 22, OK 6:9, OK 25:17 and OK 30:7. Thus, the defendant presents the defences during the preparatory stage in the district court. Amendments after that are subject to the restriction of above-mentioned preclusion rules (KKO: 2003:4; see however KKO: 2010:9). The exception is a counterclaim about set-off made in the Court of Appeal, which can be dismissed if it cannot be adjudicated without difficulty (OK 25:17.2).

V. Joinder of Claims

A. Principles

201. The Finnish law on procedure allows quite flexible joinder of both claims and parties. The joinder is considered efficient for both parties and the court, because the common grounds for claims and the common evidence can be presented in the same procedures and usually even in the same main hearing. In addition, when the claims are processed together, the risk of contradictory judgments on the basis of the same evidence is avoided. It is also acknowledged that a joinder of too many claims lead to complicated proceedings, which are difficult to master, and therefore the courts have the possibility to severe the claims from each other.

202. Both the joinder of causes (objective cumulation) and the joinder of parties (subjective cumulation) are regulated in Chapter 18 of the Code of Procedure. Under certain conditions, the joinder is mandatory (OK 18:1–5). In addition, the law gives the court a flexible margin to join the claims in other situations (OK 18:6). The joinder does not mean that every claim is processed exactly in the same way. The court has also considerable discretion to form the procedure according to the nature of the matter. The court can give a judgment on some of the claims in advance of the rest of the case (OK 24:5–6) and prepare the claims separately (OK 5:23). The court can even hold the main hearings separately for different parts of the joint matters (OK 5:30) but that is, of course, rare, because then the benefits of the joinder are lost.

203. The joinder of causes or parties is only possible when the cases could also be processed separately. Thus, the judgment in one of the cases would not have the effect of res judicata on other cases.

204. When the possibility of different judgments is excluded, that is, when the parties can only dispose of the object of the dispute together, it is required that they litigate together (necessary joinder; *litis consortium necessarium*). Most important examples of such situations are the joint administration of the estate in inheritance law and the joint ownership of property. In such cases, all the parties to the estate or all the owners have to be parties to the litigation. The court controls, when giving the summons, that all the parties are summoned and, if not, gives the plaintiff the possibility to do so (KKO 2002:80).

B. Joinder of Causes

205. If the plaintiff files several claims against the (same) defendant that are based on essentially the same grounds, the claims have to be processed together (OK 18:1). The concept 'essentially the same grounds' is the same as in OK 14:1 paragraph 1 point 3 and, thus, the joint claim could also be presented later in the procedure as an amendment of the claim. Thus, the claims must be based on the same legal relationship, such as the same contract or the same cause of damages.

206. The joinder is mandatory according to OK 18:1, if the claims have been filed at the same time. Usually the claims are filed in the same summons but separate summons are also possible if the time difference between the filings is of no practical importance.

207. The joinder is only possible if the followed procedure is the same and the court has jurisdiction over both actions (OK 18:7.1). Thus, claims that fall under the jurisdiction of special courts, cannot be joined with matters in general courts or vice versa. However, claims concerning intellectual property rights in the market court can attract other claims, which normally would be under the jurisdiction of general courts.

208. Actions by the same plaintiff against the same defendant, even if they do not fulfil the strict requirements for mandatory joinder in OK 18:1, can be processed together according to OK 18:6 which gives the court discretion in joinder. For example, claims based on similar contracts between the same parties are often processed together and so are claims based on different contracts that are parts of the whole matter.

209. Counteraction is processed in the same proceedings with the plaintiff's original action if it is based on the same or a connected matter as the original action. Also, if the counterclaim may be set-off against the original claim, they are processed together (OK 18:3).

210. As a counteraction, the defendant can, for example, file a declaratory action claiming that the alleged contractual relationship does not exist. The requirement that the counteraction must be based on the substantial connection between the actions is somewhat wider than that of essentially same ground in OK 14:1 and OK 18:1 and 2.

211. Also, the set-off against the plaintiff's claim can act as the basis for a counteraction. The debt that is invoked for the set-off as the basis of a counteraction does not need to be connected to the original action.

212. The same grounds that can be the basis for the counteraction can usually be invoked as a defence against the original action. The advantage of a counteraction is that even if the plaintiff's action is dismissed, the defendant can get a verdict against the plaintiff.

213. The joinder of the counteraction is mandatory when filed during the preparatory stage of the trial (OK 18:7.2). The same court that has jurisdiction over the original action also has jurisdiction over the counteraction (OK 10:7a.1).

C. Joinder of Parties

214. If the plaintiff files actions, which are based essentially on the same grounds, at the same time against several defendants, these actions are to be processed together (OK 18:2). Typically, a damage caused by several defendants is processed jointly. Also, if several plaintiffs file actions against one defendant, or against several defendants, and the actions are based essentially on the same grounds and they are filed at the same time, they are processed jointly. If several plaintiffs have suffered damage caused by the same defendant, as may be the case in an environmental damage case, the actions are processed jointly.

215. The joinder is mandatory according to OK 18:2 if the actions are filed at the same time. The time difference in filing should be quite small and of no practical importance. In addition, the procedure to be followed should be the same and the court should have jurisdiction over all parties in the case. In cases of mandatory joinder according to OK 18:2, if a court has jurisdiction over one of the defendants, it also has jurisdiction over all the other defendants (OK 10:10 section 2). This rule covers the dispositive jurisdictions in Chapter 10. A prorogation contract or an arbitration contract, however, is not valid against those who are not parties to the contract (KKO:2014:3).

216. Sometimes, the outcome of a trial has a disadvantageous effect on a third party. For example, when two or more persons are liable for the same debt, a verdict against one of them gives him a right of recourse against the other debtors or sureties, or at least has notable evidentiary value in a subsequent action against him. Another example is an insurance provider whose liability is dependent on the trial against the insured. OK 18:5.2 gives the third party a possibility to become a party in the trial under such circumstances. OK 18:5.1 gives the parties in the original trial a possibility to draw the third party into the trial. The joinder of the actions in these cases is mandatory if the action is filed during the preparation stage of the first trial. The rule of *forum connexitatis* applies.

217. If a third party wants to claim that he has a better right, such as ownership, to the object of the dispute, this third party must file a suit against both parties of the original dispute (*pääväliintulo*). Such an action is processed together with the original action (OK 18:4). Joinder is mandatory if the third party files the action during the preparatory stage of the trial.

218. Even if the joinder is not legally mandatory, the court has a rather wide discretion to join actions between the same parties and even 'different' parties (OK 18:6) if it is in the interest of the clarification of the matter. Thus, for example, actions by several plaintiffs against the same defendant based on similar contracts, as can be the case in consumer contracts, can be processed together if the actions have essential evidence that is common to all cases. Also, claims by the same plaintiff based on similar contracts against several defendants could be processed together, but this rarely happens. The exceptional forum rule (*forum connexitatis*) in OK 10:10.2 does not apply to discretionary joinder according to OK 18:6 and 18:7.

219. In both mandatory and discretionary joinder of parties, each party is responsible for his procedural actions and the outcome in each suit can be different. Thus, the case can end with a judgment by default against some of the defendants, while it proceeds to the main hearing against other defendants.

Chapter 3. Sanctions on Procedural Irregularities

§1. Formal Requirements

220. If the application for summons is deficient, the court will notify the plaintiff and grant him a possibility to amend the application (OK 5:5). If the plaintiff declines to do so or if the application still cannot be the basis for a trial after amendment, the application for summons is dismissed (OK 5:6).

221. Generally in dispositive matters, a party who fails to comply with his responsibilities in the trial runs the risk of a default judgment. If the defendant does not respond to the summons or a later notice to respond or to attend to a hearing, a default judgment against the defendant can be given. The respondent is even obliged to state the grounds for denial of the plaintiff's claim, with the risk of default judgment (OK 5:13–14; OK 12:10; OK 12:13). A default judgment against the plaintiff is also possible if the plaintiff fails to respond to a notice by the court or to appear in a hearing (OK 12:10; OK 12:12).

The sanction for failure to appear at a hearing, when requested to appear personally, is a fine. If the court deems it necessary to hear the party personally, it can order that the party be brought to court.

§2. Time Limits

222. Some time limits, such as the deadline for appeal or bringing an action in some cases, are fixed in the law (see Part IV Chapter 4 § 2). The court sets most intra-procedural time limits during the trial. The most important sanction for the dismissal of such time limits is, besides dismissal and default judgment, the preclusion, that is, claims, grounds and evidence presented after the time limit has passed, are not taken into account by the court.

Part IV. Proceedings

Chapter 1. Introduction: Preparatory Stage and Main Hearing

223. In the preparation of the 1993 reform, the funnel metaphor was frequently used to illustrate the flow of cases through the civil procedure. All cases entered the procedure in the same way (by summons), simple cases were decided on documents, a number of cases were decided after a preparatory hearing and only the most demanding cases went to the main hearing. Thus, the flow of cases became narrower with each step in the procedure and an illustration of the procedure looked like a funnel.

Figure 2 Civil Procedure

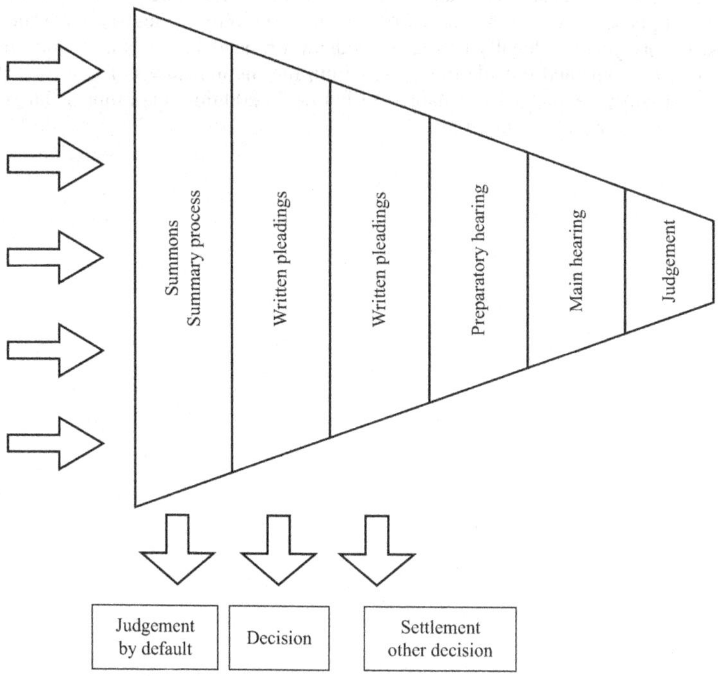

224. The mouth of the funnel was quite wide because a separate proceeding for the collection of undisputed monetary claims (*maksamismääräys*; payment order) was abolished in the 1993 reform. These kinds of collection claims are now decided in civil procedure on the basis of a summary action. The decision is usually made on documents in the preparatory stage of the trial. Only if the claim is disputed, the summary proceeding is transformed to an ordinary civil proceeding. In 2013, out of almost 440,000 civil actions in the district courts, almost 99% were decided on documents. The majority of those were undisputed collection claims.

225. Only 5,000 civil cases proceeded to oral hearings in district courts in 2013. Half of those were decided after a preparatory hearing and half after a main hearing (Court Statistics 2013). The number of oral hearings in civil cases declined after the 1993 reform from over 10,000 in 1995 to its present level during the latter half of the 1990s. Also, in a long perspective the number of civil cases seems to be low (Ervasti 2009).

226. The civil procedure is divided into two distinct stages: the preparatory stage and the main hearing. The preparatory stage can be divided into three parts: the initiation of the trial, the preparation on the documents and the preparatory hearing.

227. As the preparatory stage is part of the civil procedure, there is no formal pre-trial phase. However, mediation has been favoured by the legislators during the past twenty years. A legally regulated mediation procedure exists now both inside the district court and outside the court within the municipalities. These mediation systems will be explained in Chapter XI below. In addition, the Finnish Bar Association has a mediation program.

Chapter 2. Proceedings in First Instance

§1. Adversary Proceedings

I. Ordinary Proceedings

A. *Introduction of the Claim*

1. Registration by the Court

228. The application for summons is filed in the district court, which registers it on the day of filing. The date of filing is decisive for the effect of *lis pendens.*

229. When the claim is a pecuniary payment backed by a document, the application for summons can be filed electronically according to the Act on Electronic Services and Communication in the Public Sector (*Laki sähköisestä asioinnista viranomaistoiminnassa* 13/2003; telefax was allowed already in 1992; KKO:1992:64). It is required, however, that the person who files electronically can authenticate the document with an electronic signature according to the Act on Electronic Signatures (*Laki sähköisistä allekirjoituksista* 14/2003). Individuals can use their bank authentication. Companies can obtain a specific authentication for the courts. In practice, the big institutional creditor-plaintiffs use electronic summons. The electronic processing can then be used during the whole trial, including the transfer of the judgment to the enforcement agent.

230. The court fees are charged afterwards. The fees are regulated in the Court Fee Act (Tuomioistuinmaksulaki 1455/2015; in force 1 January 2016). The cost for the service of the summons is included in the court fee.

2. Notice

231. The court issues the summons, which is then served on the defendant. In the summons, the defendant is exhorted to give a written response to the summons. The defendant can also respond orally in court in special circumstances (OK 5:9).

232. In the response, the defendant states whether she admits or contests the action and presents the grounds for contesting. The defendant also lists in, as far as possible, the evidence she intends to present and what she intends to prove with each piece of evidence (OK 5:10). The defendant also makes a dilatory plea, such as a plea of want of jurisdiction. Furthermore, the defendant should make a claim for the compensation of legal costs if necessary.

233. The service of the summons is taken care of by the court. In practice, the district courts employ one or more writ servers. In civil cases, the court may also entrust the plaintiff to serve the summons (OK 11:2). This is exceptional but sometimes happened when the defendant was particularly difficult to locate but the plaintiff had some inside information about her movements. A recent amendment favours service by the plaintiff (362/2010).

234. Summons is served personally on the defendant. An attorney may receive a summons in a civil case if the power of attorney specifically empowers the attorney to do so (OK 11:16).

235. If the defendant is a legal person, the summons is served on the legal representative. The estate of a deceased person is served to its administrator or to the parties of the estate or to the party in the possession of the estate (OK 11:14).

236. The service of the summons is done: (1) through the postal service so that the defendant signs for delivery; or (2) by regular post so that the defendant returns a certificate of service before a given deadline; or (3) personally so that the writ server of the court personally serves the summons to the defendant (OK 11:3 and 11:4). In a summary proceedings, summons can also be served by phone (OK 11:3b; 362/2010). The application for summons and additional documents can be sent to the party by electronic communication, when the service is done according to the above mentioned procedures 1 and 2.

237. In civil procedure, the summons is also served by a 'subsidiary' service. If the writ server has not found a defendant, who has domicile and residence in Finland, or a person who is competent to receive the service, and there is reason to believe that the person is evading the service, the writ server can deliver the documents to a household member, who is at least 15 years of age, or to an employee of the defendant. If none of the above can be found, the service is delivered to the local police. The writ server notifies the recipient by a letter to his home address (OK 11:7). The possibility for this kind of service when the defendant had a post box in the region was subject to adjudication in KKO:2006:69.

238. If the defendant has no known domicile and residence and cannot be located, the service is done by announcements in the *Official Gazette* and in the court (OK 11:8). When the defendant was domiciled in Spain, there was a duty to inquire about her address before a service by announcement could be made (KKO:2008:48). Service through announcement can also be used when the service concerns so many parties that separate service on each of them would be unduly inconvenient. The summons in such cases are served on one of the parties and a summary of it and the name of the recipient are published in the *Official Gazette*. This procedure is rarely used.

239. If the defendant resides in another EU country, the service is delivered according to Council Regulation (EC) No. 1348/2000 of 29 May 2000 on the service in Member States of judicial and extrajudicial documents in civil or commercial matters. Finland is party to the Hague Treaty on Service of Documents in Cases and Matters of Civil or Commercial Nature (15 November 1965) and to the Nordic

Convention of 26 April 1974. The procedure according to the Hague Convention is regulated in a Decree 211/1982 and the central authority is the Ministry of Justice.

240. The service of documents other than summons is performed by post as regulated in OK 11:3. Such a service can be delivered by an ordinary letter or by phone or as electronic communication to the address given by the party (362/2010). A duty to be present at a court session is always served personally to the party (OK 11:16.4).

3. Summary Judgment

241. The case can be decided at the preparatory stage on the documents under several paragraphs (see 1.1.2.2). The court can rule an action inadmissible without granting the summons. This is possible on formal grounds if the application for a summons is so incomplete that it is not fit to be the basis for proceedings and the plaintiff fails to complete it when asked to do so (OK 5:6). The court refrains from granting the summons if the court for some reason, such as lack of jurisdiction, cannot process the case. Furthermore, the court can refuse the summons if the claim of the plaintiff is manifestly without a basis (OK 5:6; see Supreme Court KKO:2005:74).

242. The most common decision on documents is a default judgment. If the defendant fails to respond to the summons before a given deadline in a dispositive matter, the court gives a default judgment against the defendant. Even if the defendant responds to the summons and denies the claim but fails to give relevant grounds to the denial, the court can give a default judgment against the defendant (OK 5:13). However, if the action is manifestly unfounded the default judgment shall not be granted.

243. If the action is based on a promissory note, a bill of exchange or a cheque, the court gives a default judgment against the defendant if he/she has not presented either probable reasons for contesting the claim or an enforceable judgment on a debt, a negotiable promissory note, a bill of exchange or a cheque that is admissible for set-off (OK 5:14). However, if the action is manifestly unfounded, the court does not grant a default judgment.

B. Progress of Proceedings

1. Preparatory Measures

244. The purpose of the preparatory proceedings is to make clear the claims and objections of both parties as well as the grounds invoked as support for their claims. Further, the purpose is to ascertain whether the parties agree on some of the grounds and what exactly is the object of the dispute (OK 5:19). The parties also state what evidence they will present and what are the evidentiary themes attached to each piece of evidence. In addition, the court discusses the possibilities of conciliation between the parties and if appropriate, promotes and proposes a settlement in the case (OK 5:26).

245. Both the application for the summons and the defendant's response are regulated in detail by law. The defendant states in the response the procedural objections, whether she contests or admits the claim or part of the claim, the grounds for contesting the claim, presents documentary evidence and lists the witnesses and other parties she wants to hear and gives the evidentiary themes for each piece of evidence (OK 5:10). According to the law, the defendant can be requested to give the response orally in a hearing instead of in a written response, but this procedure is hardly ever used (OK 5:9).

246. In the preparation of the case, the court can ask the parties to deliver a written statement. Such a request specifies which issue the statement comments upon (OK 5:15a). In principle, only one written statement is allowed but the practice has been somewhat more flexible.

247. The court can hold a preparatory hearing; such a hearing is generally held in most disputed civil cases. The purpose of the hearing is to prepare the suit for the main hearing and to clarify the exact scope of the dispute, the evidence to be presented and the evidentiary themes. The preparatory hearing is an oral hearing; the parties are not allowed to present or to read written statements out loud. This rule does not exclude the use of documents or notes in support of the oral statement (OK 5:15c). The preparatory hearing can be hold as a telephone conference or by other communicative link when appropriate (OK 5:15d).

248. The law mentions only one session preparatory hearing. In practice, however, the preparatory hearing is sometimes adjourned and continued after some other preparatory measures, like obtaining documentation or settlement negotiations, have been carried out. The preparation of a case can also be differentiated so that separable parts of the case are each prepared separately according to OK 5:23. This provision gives the court a flexible tool for appropriate preparation of large lawsuits.

249. One of the purposes of the preparation is to ensure that all evidence can be presented at the main hearing. Therefore, the court makes decisions about appointing an expert, obtaining documents, inspection on-site or other such measures during the preparation (OK 5:25). The court shall either order a party or a third party to present the evidence, such as a document, or to take measures itself to hold an inspection on-site or, exceptionally, to hear a witness before the main hearing.

250. The preparation is the responsibility of the judge to whom the case has been allocated. This judge also has the competence to make all the necessary decisions during the preparation (OK 2:5.1 point 2). The role of the judge in preparation is active because the court prepares the case so that the main hearing can be continuous (OK 5:21).). An active role by the judge was expected in clarification of the grounds in KKO:2007:52 and 1998:117.

251. The parties present their claims, grounds and evidence during the preparation with the risk of preclusion (OK 5:20, 6:9, 13:2). The court sets a final date, after which the presentation of additional materials is precluded (OK 5:22).

252. If a party does not appear at a hearing or does not give a written statement, a default judgment can be given against that party (OK 5:27; OK 12:10). A default judgment is given after a request by the other party, under the condition that the claim is not manifestly unfounded. If a party, ordered to appear at a hearing personally under threat of a fine, does not appear, such an order will be given again or that party can be ordered to be brought to the court (OK 12:19).

253. The court makes a summary of the claims, grounds and evidence presented in the case. The summary is presented either before the preparatory hearing, in which case it is given orally, or at the end of the preparation. In any case, the parties have a right to comment on the summary (OK 5:24).

254. The court has a duty to promote a settlement between the parties in dispositive matters. If appropriate, the court can even make a proposal for a settlement (OK 5:26).

2. Written Procedure

255. The case can be concluded on several grounds in the documents before the preparatory hearing. As explained above, a default judgment can be given against the defendant who declines to respond to the summons. Even in a later stage, if a party fails to respond to a request to deliver a statement, the court can give a default judgment against that party if the other party demands it (OK 5:27.1; OK 12:10). After the defendant has responded to the summons, the court can alternatively give the active party the chance to present the necessary evidence and give a judgment on the merits of the case (OK 12:11).

256. After the delivery of the summons, the court gives a judgment on the documents if the defendant admitted the claim. A judgment can be given against the plaintiff it the plaintiff renounces from the claim and admits the defendants claim (OK 5:27). The court can also confirm a settlement between the parties at the preparatory stage (OK 5:27.2). Such a confirmation has the same legal effect as a judgment (OK 20; 664/2005). These decisions can also be given after a preparatory hearing. See also Part IV, Ch 2, II.

3. Determination of the Trial Date

257. After the goals of the preparation are achieved, the court sets the date for the main hearing and gives notice to the parties and the witnesses (OK 5:28). There is no definite deadline for the main hearing but it must certainly be held without undue delay after the preparation.

258. The parties are not allowed to invoke new grounds or new evidence at the main hearing (OK 6:9). If the party makes it probable that he had a valid reason not to invoke the ground or evidence at the preparation, it is not precluded. Such a ground or evidence can also be allowed with the consent of the opposing party. The party must, however, immediately notify the court and inform it of the reason why the ground or evidence was not invoked during the preparation (OK 5:29).

259. The court can divide a case into several main hearings. This is possible if some of the claims can be judged separately either by an intermediate judgment or by a partial judgment according to OK 24:5–6.

4. Main Hearing

260. The main hearing is organized according to the principles of immediacy, concentration and orality. The principle of immediacy entails that the claims, grounds and evidence must be presented immediately to the judges who decide the case at the main hearing, which, according to the principle of concentration, cannot be interrupted. The case is to be presented orally.

261. According to the principle of immediacy, the material presented at the main hearing is the basis of the judgment (OK 24:2). Thus, even though the claims and grounds are clarified and documentary evidence collected during the preparation, they have to be presented at the main hearing (for exceptions see OK 17:56-60). The material presented during the preparation, however, is not always presented again. The main hearing starts with the court's summary of the preparation. Then the court asks whether the summary correctly presents the opinions of the parties.

262. Another aspect of the principle of immediacy is that the same judges hear the case from the beginning to the end. If a judge has an impediment to attend the trial to the end, a new main hearing must be held with a new judge (OK 6:1). If a fourth judge was present during the trial, he can take the position of the judge who was hindered from sitting on the bench, and a new hearing is avoided.

263. The parties present their case orally. The witnesses give their testimony orally (prohibition of written testimony). A witness can be heard through video contact for special reasons only (Part VII).

264. The main hearing is divided into three stages: the opening statements, the presentation of evidence and the closing arguments.

265. At the beginning of the main hearing, the judge presents the summary of the preparation (OK 6:2.1; 768/2002). Then the parties comment upon their claims, grounds and contestation as presented in the summary. If needed, further clarification by the parties is possible.

266. Then both parties shall have an opportunity to present their case. The presentation includes the presentation of relevant law and the alleged facts on which the claim is based. Usually the advocate of the party presents the case. It is also possible, though rare, for the advocate to present the legal foundations of the case and for the party to present the relevant facts. Documentary evidence is sometimes presented during the presentation of the case before the stage of proof taking. The parties should refrain from commenting upon the evidence at this stage.

267. At the beginning of the proof taking, the parties are heard about the facts without taking an oath, first the plaintiff and then the defendant. Then the witnesses are heard, first the witnesses of the plaintiff and then those of the defendant. It is also possible to hear witnesses for each evidentiary theme separately. A witness or a party can be heard again if necessary after hearing other evidence in the case. The court has the discretion to change the customary order presented here (OK 6:2).

268. At the end of the hearing, the parties make their closing arguments, first the plaintiff and then the defendant. After the closing arguments, the parties have an opportunity to comment on each other's closings.

269. The presentation of the case and the closing arguments are not documented, taped or recorded in stenography. The oral evidence is taped (OK 22:6) and the tape is then stored until a final judgment in the case is reached and in any case, for at least a six- month period (OK 22:10). The tape is not usually transcribed, only if the court decides to do so (OK 22:9).

C. *Judgment*

1. Deliberation

270. The deliberations for the judgment are held in camera immediately after the hearing or the next workday. When lay judges participate in the deliberations, the judge must explain to them the central issues and the relevant law (OK 23:2). The judges cannot disclose what is discussed during the deliberations.

271. If the members of the court disagree, there will be a vote. The members of the court vote in the order of seniority so that the junior judges vote first. If lay judges participate in the decision, they vote last. It is possible that the vote only concerns a specific issue of the decision, for example a procedural question. It is also possible, though rare, that several claims in a decision are subject to separate votes (OK 23:5).

272. In civil cases, the opinion backed by the majority of the members of the court becomes the final opinion of the court. In the event of a tie, the opinion supported by the chairperson wins. The dissenting judges write a dissenting opinion stating their reasons for disagreeing with the opinion (OK 23:6).

2. Different Kinds of Judgments

273. If several claims are processed together, the court can pass a separate judgment on a claim adjudicated separately. Such a *partial judgment* can, in principle, also concern the part of a claim that was admitted (OK 24:5). A claim for payment and a corresponding claim for set-off are, however, decided together, unless a default judgment concerning the main claim can be given according to the Chapter 5, § 14(2).

274. An *intermediate judgment* is given when the final decision of an action is dependent on the decision of another action heard in the same proceedings. The intermediate judgment is generally motivated by procedural costs. There are two types of intermediate judgments. First, one of the claims has a prejudicial effect on another claim. For example, the validity of the contract should be adjudicated before the interpretation of a contract clause is meaningful. Second, a claim consists of two parts and the decision on one of the claims is a prerequisite for the decision of the other parts. Typically, the causality and the responsibility for damage is a prerequisite for the adjudication of the amount of the damages.

275. In the first case, the court can adjourn the hearing of the case until the intermediate judgment is no longer open to appeal. In the second case, an intermediate judgment can be separately appealed only if the further hearing of the case becomes unnecessary after the intermediate judgment.

3. Formal Aspects of the Judgment

276. The *judgment (tuomio)* is the final decision of the court in the subject matter of the dispute. Other, preliminary or formal decisions of the court are called *decisions or court orders (päätös).*

277. The contents of a judgment are set out in OK 24:7, 24:15 and 30:26–27 for each instance. The judgment includes, in addition to formal requirements, an account on the claims and arguments of the parties, a list of witnesses and other evidence, the reasoning of the court, the law and legal principles on which the case was decided, and the conclusion of the court. The higher court includes an account of the procedure and decisions in the lower courts in its judgments. The names of the judges who decided the case are also given. When clarity of the judgment allows it, the account of the claims and arguments of the parties can be replaced in the district court by an attachment of the documents of the parties in the judgment. In practice, however, the district courts rarely do so in other than summary proceedings. Similarly, the appeal court and the Supreme Court can attach the judgment of the lower court to their judgment.

278. The writing of the judgment has been the subject of considerable scholarly attention after the 1993 reform. Two well-known procedural scholars, Professor Jyrki Virolainen, together with Petri Martikainen (2003), and Judge Sakari Laukkanen (2002) both dedicated a book on this subject and Judge Mika Huovila wrote a doctoral thesis on the same subject (2003). In addition, professor of procedural law Juha Lappalainen has taken a stand on the issue in several writings.

279. With the risk of over-simplification, the reason for this attention can be found in the changed role of the main hearing in the trial in the early 1990s. Before the reform, the statements of the parties and the witness testimonies were recorded in the court protocols, which were used as the basis of the deliberations for the judgment. Even if the reasoning in the judgment was scant, the parties could always look at the protocols for further guidance on the reasoning of the court.

280. After the reform, the basis for the judgment is only the material presented at the oral main hearing. The testimonies are recorded on tape but the tapes are not usually transcribed. Thus, no written document of the testimonies is made. At the same time, the need for a well-reasoned judgment has been emphasized. Therefore, the courts have felt uncertain about how much of the testimonies they should restate in their judgments. Some district court judges have solved the problem by including an account of the witness testimonies in the first part of the judgment, even if the law only mentions an account of the dispositions of the parties. Consequently, critics argue that the judgments have become too long, too detailed and often include irrelevant material. In my opinion, the legal form of judgment does not give guidance on how to present the evaluation of evidence and so the courts have solved an acute problem in a creative way.

4. Delivery of the Judgment

281. The judgment is either declared after the main hearing or given in chambers. At the end of the main hearing or other hearing concluding the trial, the court either pronounces the judgment or informs the parties of the time when the judgment is given in chambers and is obtainable from the court office. As a rule, the law stipulates that the judgment should be declared after the hearing. Then, the conclusion and the main reasons for the judgment are given (OK 24:8). If the matter was complicated, the judgment can be given in chambers fourteen days after the hearing and, for special reasons, even later. This possibility is probably used more often than intended. If the decision is given in written proceedings, the parties are notified of the date of the decision in advance. No notification of a default judgment, nor a notification to the winning party, is needed.

282. When the judgment is declared at the hearing, the written judgment must be available after two weeks if a party has made a notification of appeal and in other caseswithin thirty days (OK 24:14).

5. Res Judicata

283. The finality of judgments is conceptualized under the doctrine of res judicata. The effect of res judicata is activated when ordinary appeal is no longer possible.

284. When the judgment attains res judicata, a new proceeding on the same matter cannot be opened (negative res judicata-effect). In addition, the issue cannot be disputed in a new proceeding on another matter if the matter decided in the first judgment has relevance in the second proceeding (positive res judicata-effect). For example, if a court has already held that the defendant has acted negligently and is liable to pay damages to the claimant and the verdict has reached res judicata, these issues are not open to dispute in a new proceeding on the amount of damages.

285. Since there is no article on res judicata in the Code of Procedure, the limits of the res judicata-effect were developed in an abundant case law and discussed in legal scholarship (about the doctrine of res judicata, see Hepola 2005). Generally, the narrow concept of res judicata, defined by the material grounds for the claim, changed into to a wider concept, according to which res judicata covers all circumstances that could have been presented in the first proceeding as a ground for the same claim. Today, both the case law and the scholarship have accepted the wider concept of res judicata (Lappalainen 2012, at 737, KKO:1992:91; KKO:2001:136).

286. Res judicata-effect does not generally preclude new claims deriving from the same legal relationship (KKO: 1990:111). However, modification of claims presented in the first trial is precluded by res judicata. Generally, those claims that could have been presented at the first trial, notwithstanding the prohibition of amendment of claims, are covered by the res judicata-effect.

287. The reasoning for the judgment is not covered by the res judicata-effect. As a main rule, procedural decisions attain res judicata-effect. If an action is dismissed on a procedural ground, however, the hindrance can either be corrected or not. In the first case, the plaintiff can file a new action when the hindrance is corrected.

288. The res judicata-effect, theoretically, binds only the parties. In practice, a judgment can also have a strong evidentiary value in a subsequent suit against a third person. For example, a judgment given in an action between the creditor and the debtor against the debtor does not preclude the guarantor from presenting defences concerning the main claim (no res judicata-effect against the guarantor) but the judgment could have an evidentiary value in a case against the guarantor. A dismissal of the claim against the main debtor on the ground that the main obligation does not exist does, however, get a res judicata-effect against the guarantor. The evidentiary value of a judgment can vary from case to case but, in some cases, it can be quite strong. In family law, the decisions on the status of the parties, concerning, for example, paternity, custody, etc., have binding force *inter omnes*.

6. Interpretation and Rectification of Judgments

289. The Finnish law does not recognize an action which would enable a party to seek clarification of a judgment from the court. However, an extraordinary recourse to the higher court is possible if a judgment is so unclear and imperfect that it is impossible to know what has been decided (OK 31:1-2). The higher court cannot correct the judgment but the matter is usually redirected back to the court that gave the judgment in the first place.

290. The chair of the court can correct a typing or computation error and another similar error in the judgment according to OK 24:10. If appropriate, the parties are heard before the correction is made. Such rectification is marked on the judgment or, if this is not possible, the parties are given a corrected copy of the judgment.

291. The judgment can also be supplemented if the court has dismissed to decide on one of the claims (OK 24:11). The party must request a supplement within fourteen days after the judgment was given.

7. Penalty in Case of Non-compliance

292. There is no criminal offence related to non-compliance with a judgment. The offences in Criminal Code Chapter 15 Offences against the administration of justice cover false statements and other misdeeds during the trial but not the non-compliance of the judgment. Non-compliance with a civil judgment usually leads to enforcement proceedings (Part IX Chapter 2).

II. Provisional Proceedings Without a Main Hearing

293. Until 2002, the main hearing was always held before a judgment could be given in a disputed civil case. The reform in 2002 (HE 32/2001) made it possible to give a judgment on the documents even in a disputed civil case (OK 5:27a; 768/2002). If witnesses or other persons are heard for evidence, the case always goes to a main hearing. But, if the facts are not disputed or the only evidence put forward is documentary evidence (HE 32/2001, 54), the case can be decided on the documents during the preparation. Such a decision requires that both parties have consented not to have a hearing. It has to be noted that after a preliminary hearing, a judgment cannot be given according to OK 5:27a but that the case goes to the main hearing.

§2. Default Proceedings

294. A special summary process for the recovery of debts (*maksamismääräys*) was abolished during the 1993 reform. Now such simple recovery cases are processed in the written preparatory stage of the civil procedure. The Code of Procedure includes a few special provisions for the efficient processing of such claims.

295. In default proceedings the application for summons, like most other trial documents, can be filed electronically according to the Act on Electronic Services and Communication in the Public Sector In practice, the big institutional creditor-plaintiffs use electronic summons. In 2008, two-thirds of the summons were filed electronically (Niemi, Väkiparta & Tarkkala 2009, 77).

296. Usually the default judgment is given when the defendant has failed to respond to the summons (OK 5:13). Even if the defendant responds and denies the claim but does not present any grounds to the denial or presents only grounds that are manifestly irrelevant for the denial, the court shall give a default judgment. It is not necessary that the plaintiff specifically ask for a default judgment. A default judgment is not given if the claim is manifestly unfounded. The Supreme Court held in KKO:2015:60 that in summary action against a consumer an excessive default interest claim (annual rate of 118%, which was not clearly stated in the documentation for the credit) was manifestly unfounded. Based on the European Court of Justice case law, the Supreme Court held that the district court had the power to dismiss the claim on its own motion, even if the consumer defendant had not responded to the summons (see also Vaitoja 2014).

297. If the plaintiff's claim is based on a negotiable note, a bill of exchange or a check, the court shall give a default judgment against the defendant unless the defendant has invoked reasonable grounds to support her denial or presented a final judgment, a negotiable promissory note, a bill of exchange or a check that can be used for set-off (OK 5:14). Also, in this case the plaintiff need not specifically ask for a default judgment. Also later in the trial, if a party fails to respond to a request to deliver a statement, the court can give a default judgment against that party if the other party requests it (OK 5:27.1; OK 12:10).

298. A judge does not necessarily handle the default judgment based on a summary judgment. Young lawyers who take their court training (clerkship) in the district court, and other personnel of the court who have obtained the necessary education, can also give default judgments (The District Court Act §§ 17 and 19).

§3. Ex Parte Proceedings

299. Ex parte proceedings that would be processed without hearing the defendant are not generally known in Finland. However, a preliminary injunction can be given without hearing the defendant (see Part IX Chapter 1). In addition, if the defendant is not reached for the delivery of summons, there are specific rules for the instigation of the trial (see Part IV Chapter 2 §1 IA).

Chapter 3. Review Proceedings

§1. General Principles

300. The remedies are divided into ordinary and extraordinary remedies. Ordinary remedies are available during a short time frame after the judgment is given. The judgment does not get the effect of res judicata if ordinary remedies are used. The ordinary remedy to the decisions and judgments of the district court is to appeal to the Court of Appeal. The ordinary remedy to the decisions and judgments of the appeal courts is to appeal to the Supreme Court.

301. After the judgment has become *res judicata*, that is, after the time for appeal is over, it can be overturned only for exceptionally weighty reasons through extraordinary remedies. The extraordinary remedies are the annulment of the judgment for procedural error (*tuomiovirhekantelu*), the reversal of a final judgment (*tuomionpurku*) and the restoration of expired time limit (*menetetyn määräajan palautus*).

302. In addition, there are a number of remedies that fall between ordinary and extraordinary remedies. The most important of these is the right of the party, against whom a judgment by default is given, to apply for reversal in the same court that gave the default judgment. The deadline for application of such reversal is thirty days from the time when the party was notified of the default judgment (OK 12:15–17; KKO:2008:48).

§2. Appeal

I. Ordinary Appeal to the Court of Appeal

303. The decisions and judgments of the district court are appealed to the Court of Appeal and its decisions, in turn, are appealed to the Supreme Court. The review is appellative; both adjudication of law and of facts can be appealed. From October 2015, appeal is subject to leave in civil matters (about appeal Jokela 2010).

304. The decisions concerning the procedure are subject to appeal but, as a rule, the appeal is made in connection with the appeal of the final judgment of the district court in the matter (OK 16:3.3). As an exception, a decision, by which a judge is deemed unqualified, cannot be appealed (OK 16:3.2). If the case is deemed inadmissible on the grounds of an incident, this decision can be appealed (OK 16:3.1).

305. The parties may make an agreement not to appeal a decision in a dispositive civil case. Such an agreement must be made in writing and pertain to a specific dispute or to the eventual disputes arising from a given legal relationship (OK 25:2).

306. The appeal requires the party to make a declaration of intent to appeal within seven days after the judgment or the decision was given (OK 25:5). The declaration of intent to appeal is made orally, in writing or electronically to the district dcourt that gave the verdict.

307. The appeal must be made within thirty days after the verdict or decision (OK 25:12.1). If the party, which gave a declaration of appeal, has a valid reason, it can ask the district court to prolong the deadline for appeal (OK 25:13.1). A prolongation can be granted in big and complicated cases. The appeal is filed in the district court, which sends it together with the documents of the case to the Court of Appeal (OK 25:18). The appeal is adjudicated normally, even if it is erroneously filed in the Court of Appeal (OK 25:19).

308. The content of the appeal petition is regulated in OK 25:15 and the petition specifies, in addition to the appealed decision, which parts of the decision should be changed, how it should be changed and how the reasoning of the district court is erroneous according to the view of the appellant. The purpose of this provision is to help the appellants and their lawyers in relating the appeal petitions to the judgment of the lower court and to help specify their request for change.

309. Furthermore, the appellant indicates what evidence is invoked in the appeal court and, if new evidence is put forward, why it was not presented in the district court. In addition, the appellant should request that the Court of Appeal hold a main hearing if the appellant deems it necessary.

310. The party cannot invoke a new circumstance or new evidence, that is, evidence that was not presented in the district court, unless the party makes it probable that he was not able to invoke it previously or that he had a justifiable reason for not doing so (OK 25:17; case law; see KKO:2003:4; KKO:2006:54; KKO 2004:70; KKO:1997:23). New claims are not allowed in the Court of Appeal, with the exception for set-off, which is admissible if it can be handled without undue difficulty (OK 25:17.2).

311. The rule of *nulla reformatio in pejus* is followed. Consequently, the appeal court can only change a judgment or a decision within the frame of the petition of appeal. In principle, both parties should appeal before the deadline for appeal and subject to the declaration of intent to appeal. The opposing party has, however, a right to counter-appeal within two weeks after the deadline for appeal (OK 25:14a). Counter appeal is dependent on the appeal and it expires if the appeal is withdrawn or declared inadmissible (OK 25:14b). In case KKO:2006:2 the appeal concerned only legal expenses; the Supreme Court allowed counter-appeal to open also the main claims on the reduction of the price.

312. The preparation of the case is regulated in Chapter 26 §§ 1b to 19 of the Code of Procedure. If not stipulated otherwise, the rules on the preparatory stage in the district court (Chapter 5 of the Code of Procedure) are followed.

313. The appeal is subject to leave (386/2015). The appeal court grants the leave. It does not give an opinion on the merits of the case if the leave is dismissed (KKO:2013:4).

314. Before Oct 2015, the leave was only required if the value of interest (value of loss) in appeal court was below EUR 10.000.

315. The leave is granted if (1) the correctness of the judgment is in doubt (ground of reversal); (2) the decision of the district court cannot be assessed without a leave (ground for reassessment); or (3) the case has prejudicial value (precedent) or (4) there are other weighty reasons (weighty reasons). The leave may concern only one part of the case (OK 26A:11).

316. The leave was introduced in 2010 and came into force 1 January 2011. Before that, a system called screening was in force between 2003–2010, producing a rich case law and a vivid discussion by legal scholars and judges (Nylund 2006). Case law has been abundant also after the reform. Most cases from the Supreme Court, however, concern criminal procedure. In the Supreme Court, most of the cases have concerned the ground of reversal (1), that is, correctness of the judgment of the district court. In civil cases, a question of law has been the ground for leave in KKO:2012:44 (economic information in the sale contract of an apartment and its bearing on the outcome of the case) and in KKO:2014:4, which also was deemed to have precedent value (termination of a lease when the contract included an option to continue after a fixed term).

317. In questions of fact and evidence, the leave should only be granted if there are valid reasons to doubt the assessment of the district court. Such a case was KKO:2012:26, in which the dispute was over a mistake in a bank transfer and the Supreme Court deemed that the appellant had not been able to question the assessment of the evidence produced by the defendant bank.

318. The Court of Appeal decides on the leave in a quorum of three judges. The leave is granted if one of the judges supports it (OK 25A:18). The court must consider all grounds for leave (OK 25A.17.1).

319. The proceedings in the Court of Appeal are either written or oral. First, the opposing party is requested to present its written defence (OK 26:3; KKO:2009:29). If the proceedings are written, a referendary – that is, a junior member of the legal staff of the court– presents the case to the panel of three judges (OK 26:12). The majority of appeals are handled on the documents.

320. The main hearing must be held if a party requests it or when it is necessary for the evaluation of the evidence. However, even if a party has requested a main hearing, the request can be dismissed if there is no need to reconsider oral (witness and party) testimony and the main hearing is also in other respects unnecessary (OK 26:14). In KKO:2012:43 a main hearing was deemed necessary in a custody case on the request of the mother who had lost the case in the district court. The Supreme

Court underlined the significance of the case for the parties and the nature of the evidence.

321. The Court of Appeal cannot overturn the decision of the district court on the basis of the re-evaluation of the credibility of oral testimony without holding a main hearing and hearing the testimony itself (OK 26:16). The same applies to an inspection at site. The Court of Appeal cannot change the evaluation of facts of the district court based on the inspection it made, unless the Court of Appeal makes an inspection itself (OK 26:15.2). In addition, a main hearing is held if a new oral testimony is presented in the Court of Appeal (OK 26:15.3). However, such a re-evaluation is allowed if the testimony cannot be heard any more (OK 26:16).

II. Appeal to the Supreme Court

322. The appeal from the Court of Appeal to the Supreme Court requires a leave by the Supreme Court. A leave is allowed only on specific grounds. In cases in which the Court of Appeal is the first instance, an appeal to the Supreme Court is not subject to leave (OK 30:2.2).

323. The leave of appeal may be granted:

(a) if it would be important to have a decision by the Supreme Court for the application of the law in similar cases or for the consistency of the case law (precedent);
(b) for special reasons, for instance if a procedural or other error in the handling of the case would lead to the reversal or annulment of the judgment; or
(c) for another weighty reason.

324. It is also possible to appeal directly from the district court to the Supreme Court, bypassing the court of appeal (OK Chapter 30a). Such an appeal also requires a leave from the Supreme Court. The leave can be granted only on the basis of the prejudicial value of the case. Both parties must give their permission to such direct appeal. If the leave is not granted, the decision of the district court sustains.

325. The party who wants to use the direct appeal must give a notice about it when giving the declaration of intent to appeal. As an attachment the appellant must have consent to direct appeal from the opposing party.

326. The most usual ground for leave is precedent. The Supreme Court has often given precedents on new laws where established case law is found lacking. Also, a precedent is given if legislation gives the courts discretion in the application of the law. Furthermore, if the Courts of Appeal have given different decisions to the same legal problem, the Supreme Court should give a precedent in the matter. In some situations, the case law needs to be reconsidered through a precedent.

327. The deadline for requesting a leave to appeal and lodging the appeal is sixty days from decision of the Court of Appeal (OK 30:5). The appeal must state both the grounds for the leave to appeal and the grounds for the change of the judgment.

328. The appellant and the respondent may not invoke new grounds or new evidence in the Supreme Court unless the appellant makes it probable that he was not able to invoke it previously or that he had a justifiable reason for not doing so (OK 30:7 and 30:12). Even though the law does not set any obstacle to holding a hearing in the Supreme Court (OK 30:20), such hearings have been rare. There seems to a cautious tendency to increase oral hearing in the Supreme Court. A hearing can concern only part of the case.

§3. Extraordinary Review

I. Relief for a Substantive Defect in a Final Judgment

329. A final judgment in a civil case may be reversed on the basis of a substantial defect on the grounds regulated in OK 31:7.

330. First, the reversal is possible if a member or other employee of the court is found guilty of criminal conduct in connection with the case. Similarly, if the counsel of the party is found guilty of such conduct, the decision can be reversed. The reversal is possible if it is assumed that the conduct affected the outcome of the case.

331. Second, the use of a forged document as evidence in the case, under the condition that the person who presented the evidence knew that it was forged, can lead to the reversal of the judgment. Also, a deliberately given false statement by a witness or by an expert witness can be cause for reversal of the verdict. The reversal is possible if it is assumed that the document or the statement affected the outcome of the case.

332. Third, the appearance of new evidence or a new circumstance that probably would have lead to a different result had it been presented at the first trial can lead to reversal of a judgment. In such a situation, the applicant must make it probable that he was not able to invoke the evidence or the circumstance in the first trial or he had a valid reason for not doing so. In KKO:2012:93 the court stated that the applicant has the burden of showing that he had not been able to invoke the fact in the first proceedings.

333. Fourth, a judgment based on a manifestly wrong application of the law can be reversed. It has to be noted that a reversal based on this ground is not granted easily. The threshold is clearly higher than in ordinary appeal and the applications are not often successful. However, the manifestly wrong application of the law is the most commonly used ground for reversal. There are a few cases in which manifestly wrong decisions in adoption cases have been subject to reversal proceedings and the best interest of the child has been considered (KKO:2005:64 and

KKO:2014:19). The decisions of the European Courts have in some cases led to reversal of a judgment (KKO:2007:34; in KKO:2007:35 the time limit for reversal had passed).

334. Fifth, if a person has been handled under a wrong name and false identity in a trial, the judgment can be reversed and corrected (OK 31:11).

335. The application for reversal must be made within one year after the applicant was informed about the circumstance that forms the ground for the application (OK 31:10). If the application for the reversal of the judgment is based on criminal conduct, the time limit is counted from the res judicata of the verdict, in which the person was convicted of the crime. If the application is based on a manifestly wrong application of the law, the time limit is one year after the judgment. A judgment cannot, in any case, be reversed after five years have passed from the judgment. The exception is a correction of the judgment been given in the name of a wrong person, which may be corrected notwithstanding these time limits.

336. The application for reversal is made to the Supreme Court (OK 31:12). The applicant must be represented by a legal counsel (OK 15:1.4). If relief is granted, the Supreme Court usually annuls the judgment and orders how and when a retrial in the lower court must be instigated. The Supreme Court also corrects the judgment itself when appropriate.

II. Relief for Procedural Error

337. A grave procedural error can be ground for the annulment of a judgment. Such grave errors are defined in the Chapter 31 § 1 of the Code of Procedure.

338. First, if the court did not have the required quorum or if a judge was disqualified from the bench or if the court should have had declared the case inadmissible out of its own volition, for example, for lack of jurisdiction, the judgment should be annulled. However, error in territorial jurisdiction is not a ground for annulment (OK 31:1.2).

339. Second, if a person who did not receive a service was convicted or a person who was not heard suffers inconvenience of the judgment otherwise, the judgment should be annulled.

340. Third, a judgment that is so confusing or defective that it is not apparent, what has been decided, should be annulled. In principle, the judgments should be so clear that they can be enforced without any difficulty. In practice, this ground is almost never invoked.

341. Fourth, another procedural error can lead to the annulment of the judgment if it is assumed that it has essentially affected the outcome of the case. The annulment decisions in civil matters are rare. The procedural error was the ground for annulment in KKO:2007:86, in which an order of enforcement in a child custody case was processed as undisputed, notwithstanding the mother's objection.

342. The application for relief for a procedural error in the district court should be filed to the Court of Appeal and for a procedural error in the Court of Appeal or the Supreme Court to the last-mentioned court (OK 31:2). The applicant must be represented by a legal counsel (OK 15:1.4).

343. The application for relief for a procedural error must be made within six months after the judgment. If a person who was not served or heard is convicted, an application for relief must be made within six months after he became aware of the judgment. If the relief is granted, the case is referred to the Court in which the error has been made (OK 31:6).

III. Restoration of Expired Time

344. If someone has not been able to declare intent to appeal, to lodge an appeal, to file a complaint or to undertake another action in a trial before a deadline and he had a legal obstacle or an otherwise compelling reason for not doing so, this person can file a petition for a new deadline (OK 31:17). A petition for a new deadline is made in writing to the court of appeal when it concerns a judgment of the district court and otherwise to the Supreme Court. The deadline for the petition is thirty days of the termination of the excuse referred to in section 17 and, at the latest, within one year after the deadline (OK 31:18). If the applicant is successful, he is granted a new deadline for filing.

345. An abundance of case law has clarified what deadlines are procedural and what can be restored and what cannot. For example, a time limit for the reversal of judgment cannot be restored (KKO:2003:20).

Part V. Incidents

Chapter 1. Challenge of Judges

§1. Disqualification of the Judge in a Case

346. A judge is disqualified from a specific case when he has such a close connection with the parties of the case that his impartiality is in danger. The situations in which a judge is disqualified are enumerated in the law (OK Chapter 13; 441/2001). The lay judges are subject to the same disqualifications as ordinary judges (OK 13:2.1).

347. The judge is disqualified to handle a case if he (OK 13:4):

- is party in the case;
- is or has been representative or advocate in the case;
- is or has been a witness or an expert in the case;
- can expect special advantage or disadvantage from the case;
- is director or a member of a corporate council (or in a similar position) in a company that is party in the case;
- is in a decision-making position in a public body that is party in the case; and
- has employment or a similar relationship to a party that can endanger his impartiality.

348. A disqualification can be based on an adversarial relationship in another case, which has nothing to do with the case in question (OK 13:6). Appeals against the State or other public community, for example in tax matters, do not disqualify the judge. Also, a judge who is a party in a similar case (but with a different opponent) is disqualified if there is reason to suspect that his impartiality would be at risk (OK 13:7.1).

349. Furthermore, a judge who handled the case previously in another court, on another board, some other body or in arbitration, is disqualified (OK 13:7.1). If the judge handled the case previously in the same court and an appeal court overturned the case and sent it back to the original court, special consideration to the circumstances is required (OK 13:7.2; see KKO:2004:42: no disqualification because the grounds for the applications were different; KKO:2000:104: a judge who had given an order of seizure in the preparatory stage of the trial was not disqualified from sitting in the main trial).

350. Finally, even a circumstance that has not been mentioned in the law can lead to disqualification (OK 13:7.3). According to case KKO:2008:95, a lay judge should have disqualified himself as he had stated an opinion on the suspect's guilt before a criminal trial was initiated.

351. The judge is also disqualified if one of his close relatives is in one of the above-mentioned positions. The closest relatives – that is spouse, children, grandchildren, parents, grandparents, siblings, and other especially close persons and their spouses – are, as a main rule, treated in the same way as the judge (OK 13:3). In KKO:2000:49 the spouse of the judge was a bank employee, with the right to sign for the bank. The judge was disqualified from a case of debt adjustment, in which the bank was one of the creditors. If other relatives, as also enumerated in law, and the relatives of the judge's spouse, are parties, representatives or witnesses in the case, the judge is disqualified, but the more indirect disqualifications do not apply in relation with these persons.

§2. PROCEDURE

352. In principle, the disqualifications are taken into account ex officio, notwithstanding a motion by a party. Each judge has the obligation to observe his own impartiality.

353. In practice, the parties often make motions to disqualify a judge. Such a motion must be made immediately after the party was informed of the judges in the case or immediately after the party was informed of the ground for disqualification. The party cannot invoke a disqualification ground after the judgment in the case is given, unless the party shows that he had a valid reason for not doing so earlier (OK 13:8).

354. The motion is decided by the same court, but, as a main rule, not by the judge concerned. The district court is competent in the quorum of one judge. In the appeal court and the Supreme Court normal quorum rules are followed. The judge can participate in the decision-making on an objection about his disqualification if the court is not competent without him and another judge cannot participate without undue delay. The judge can also dismiss an objection to disqualify him if the objection is manifestly unfounded (OK 13:9).

355. After a disqualification, a judge only makes decisions that have no bearing on the outcome of the trial. In practice, the judge sets the date for a further hearing or other procedural measures in the case.

356. A decision, by which an objection to disqualify a judge is accepted, cannot be appealed. If an objection is dismissed, an appeal is possible. Such an appeal is made together with the appeal for the main issue. The court can, however, decide that a separate appeal is allowed and postpone further hearing in the case until the higher court decides on the appeal (OK 16:3.3).

Chapter 2. Intervention

§1. Participation in the Trial

357. The institution of intervention covers situations in which some other person than a party wants to participate in the ongoing trial. Thus, intervention is to be distinguished from the joinder of actions, according to which several parties or several claims can be processed in the same trial, and from the necessary joinder, according to which several persons can only process together.

358. In principle, the attitude towards third-party intervention is negative. For example, interventions by interest groups (*amicus briefs*) or by persons who have a similar legal interest in another case and are worried about the prejudicial effect of the trial are not known in the Finnish law. From the flexible rules on joinder follows that those whose rights will be touched by the judgment can bring an action against a party and be joined in the trial. The institution of intervention is also flexible and it is not known how common it is in the lower courts.

§2. Ordinary and Independent Intervention

359. An intervenient (*sivuväliintulija*) does not make his own claims but supports one of the parties (OK 18:8–10). In doing so, the intervenient has a legal interest of his own. It is possible that the intervenient has the alternative to bring an action in the same issue and claims joinder to the lawsuit at his disposal. This possibility does not preclude intervention if the intervenient chooses to do so.

360. The legal interest of the intervenient can be, first, that he will be bound by the judgment (independent intervenient; OK 18:10.2). Examples of such interventions could be a bankrupt debtor in a suit instigated by the bankrupt estate or a subtenant in a lawsuit between the owner and the tenant over the possession of the premises. In KKO:2007:96 an executor of an estate was held as an intervenient in a case concerning his replacement.

361. Second, the intervention can be based on the evidentiary value of the judgment on the right of the intervenient (OK 18:10.1; ordinary intervenient). For example, if the employee has caused damage in the work, the employer can intervene in the trial against the employee because the employer can be liable for such damage (Tort Liability Act (*Vahingonkorvauslaki*412/1975) 7:5). A leading case is KKO:2008:30 in which a creditor requested the right to intervene in an action on payment of debt between another creditor and the debtor, claiming that the purpose of the action was to hinder the payment to intervenient-creditor. The right to intervene was denied.

362. Both types of intervention are possible at any stage of the trial, even in the main hearing or in the Court of Appeal. In some cases, the intervenient is notified of the trial according to the law (*litis denuntiatio*), but an intervenient can also intervene on his own initiative. An ordinary intervenient cannot dispose of any part of the action, but he can present evidence and support the claims of the party (OK 18:10.1). An independent intervenient, however, has the same rights as a party (OK 18:10.2). An independent intervenient can even appeal the judgment.

Chapter 3. Withdrawal and Termination of an Action

363. The plaintiff can withdraw the action until the defendant has responded. After the response, the defendant can request adjudication of the case, even if the plaintiff wants to withdraw.

364. A withdrawal by consent is possible if both parties fail to appear at a hearing. Then the case is withdrawn from the court (struck off the docket). The withdrawal has no res judicata-effect and the parties can file the application for summons again later on if they like.

365. The action can be terminated or dismissed on a procedural ground if one of the procedural preconditions (*prosessinedellytys*) is missing. The procedural requirements can be, however, either reparable or irreparable. In the first instance, either the court has the responsibility to correct the problem or the party is given the opportunity to cure it. For example, the court corrects ex officio procedural objections concerning the court, such as disqualification of the judge. Similarly, failures in the service of the summons are corrected by a new service.

366. Some of the procedural requirements, for example many rules on venue, are dispositive, that is, they are only observed if the defendant makes an objection. Such an objection must be made when the defendant first responds in the trial (OK 16:1). Mandatory procedural requirements must also be observed later on, at any stage of the trial.

Chapter 4. Postponement of the Main Hearing

367. The principle of concentration requires that the main hearing is uninterrupted (OK 6:5). Therefore, the possibilities to postpone or to adjourn the main hearing are very limited.

368. If the court notices at the beginning of a main hearing that it cannot be carried on uninterrupted, for example, because a core witness has failed to appear, the hearing is cancelled and rescheduled (OK 6:6). Even if the main hearing is rescheduled, a witness or other person can be heard if he cannot attend the new hearing without undue inconvenience (OK 17:56; 732/2015).

369. Once the main hearing has started, it continues for several days, at least three days every week. The main hearing is only adjourned for special reasons. The adjournment normally cannot exceed fourteen days, and for a special reason an adjournment up to forty-five days can be accepted. (OK 6:10–11). In practice, the courts have successfully avoided adjournments in civil cases.

Chapter 5. Substitution of the Parties

§1. General Substitution

370. General substitution occurs when all the property rights and relations of a party are transferred to another legal subject. Typically, the death of a natural person, fusion or change of legal form of a legal person and bankruptcy cause a general substitution. The successor of the party is informed of the trial and given appropriate time to consider whether he wants to continue the trial. If the successor wants to continue the trial, he will have the same rights and duties as the original party.

371. If the trial concerns the personal rights of the parties, for example divorce, the trial is discontinued after the death of a party. An exception is the paternity trial.

§2. Special Substitution

372. Special substitution takes place when the object of the trial is transferred to another person during the trial.

373. If special substitution takes place on the plaintiff's side, the new plaintiff has the right to become a party to the trial. The earlier dispositions of the original plaintiff bind the new plaintiff, and the original plaintiff can be liable for the costs that are accumulated before the substitution (OK 12:5a.1 and 21:10.1). The substitution on the defendant's side requires that the plaintiff accept the change of defendant (OK 12:5a.2). The opposing party has a right to require that the transferee join the procedure (OK 12:5a.3).

Part VI. Legal Aid and Legal Costs

Chapter 1. Legal Aid

374. Originally, legal aid was given by private attorneys, whose costs could be covered by the State. Of course, such legal aid was only meant for the poor. The first municipal Legal Aid Act was enacted in 1973, expanding the scope of cost free procedure and establishing the municipal legal aid offices. At the beginning of 2000s, the legal aid offices were transferred to the State organization and the two systems of legal aid were brought under the same law. The purpose of this reform was to extend legal aid, which was mostly used by the poor, to low-income clients and to facilitate the possibility to get partial legal aid (about the Finnish legal aid system Rosti, Niemi & Lasola 2008).

375. The Legal Aid Act gives relief from the court fees and covers the evidentiary costs, interpretation costs, cost of the representation in the court and legal advice (about translation costs: KHO:2011/1176). When the evidentiary costs are covered by the legal aid, the level of the costs and fees is determined by the State Compensation for the Witnesses Act (*Laki valtion varoista maksettavista todistelukustannuksista* 666/1972) and Decree (813/1972). The costs of representation are, however, covered only under specific conditions.

376. The legal aid is given to citizens of Finland and other EU countries, to persons who have domicile in Finland and to persons who have a case pending in a Finnish court. In international lawsuits, a party can get legal advice and, for a special reasons, other assistance (Legal Aid Act § 23). Legal aid is only given in a dispute that concerns private economic activity of the person as opposed to business (Legal Aid Act § 2).

377. Legal aid is given to persons who cannot afford legal advice. Only minor advice can be given by the public legal aid attorneys without checking the economic eligibility of the client (Legal Aid Act § 3a). The rules for eligibility for aid are regulated by a Government Decree on Legal Aid (388/2002). In principle, the client can deduct necessary living expenses of the family from his income and the surplus, that is, the available means, forms the basis for granting legal aid and for determining the part the client has to pay. If a person's disposable income is less than EUR 600, she has a right to legal aid without deductible. When her disposable income is between EUR 600 and EUR 1,300 she has to pay a deductible according to a progressive scale (Legal Aid Decree § 5). There are special rules for taking into account the assets of the client (Legal Aid Decree § 7).

378. If the client has an insurance that covers the respective costs, legal aid is only given to compensate costs that are not covered by the insurance policy (Legal Aid Act § 3b).

379. Legal aid is not given for the costs of representation in matters that are filed in the court by application. This rule excludes several family law matters from the scope of legal aid. However, legal aid can be granted for special reason, which often is the case in disputed custody cases. Legal aid is excluded if the matter has only insignificant effect on the client or if it would be otherwise inappropriate (Legal Aid Act § 7).

380. The maximum for legal aid in a case is, as a main rule, eighty hours; the court decides whether to continue the legal aid in a pending case when it exceeds eighty hours (Legal Aid Act § 5.2 as amended by Law 927/2008).

381. The request for legal aid is made to the public legal aid office, which makes the decision on granting legal aid. If the request is denied, the client can take the matter to the court, which would have jurisdiction over the material dispute if the case goes to court (Legal Aid Act §§ 11 and 24). The legal aid office has power to investigate the economic situation of the client by requesting information from tax authorities, pension foundations, insurance companies and banks (Legal Aid Act § 10).

382. The client can choose between a public legal aid attorney and a private attorney (Legal Aid Act § 8). Legal advice that is not related to a court case is basically only given by the public legal aid offices. The fees of the private attorney are confirmed by the court, in which the case is pending, or by the legal aid office. The fee for private attorneys is EUR 110 per hour (Decree on legal aid remuneration 290/2008 § 6) and at least EUR 515 per hearing in civil cases.

383. Legal aid does not change the rules of compensation of the costs of the opposing party. If the winning party has legal aid, the losing party is obliged to compensate the costs of legal aid.

Chapter 2. Legal costs

§1. Types of Costs

384. The legal costs are either court fees or party costs. The plaintiff or the appellant is obliged to pay a fee. This fee covers the service of summons and one official copy of the judgment. The court fees are regulated by the Court Fee Act (1455/2015)), supplemented by the Court Fee Decree (1755/2015).

Table 1 Court Fees 2016

Court	*Fee (EUR)*
District Court, civil matters	500
District Court, default judgment etc.	86
District Court, default judgment - filed electronically	65
District Court, summary case, disputed	250
Market Court	2000
Court of Appeal	500
Supreme Court	500

385. Party costs include the expenses for the evidence, the expenses to the party itself for the preparation of the case and appearance in court and the advocate's fee (OK 21:8). The parties are initially liable for their own costs. If a party calls a witness, that party is liable to cover the expenses for that witness. If a witness or an expert is called by the court or by both parties, they are jointly liable for the costs.

§2. Compensation of Legal Costs

386. The main rule is that the losing party is obligated to compensate for the costs of the winning party in a civil suit (OK 21:1). In indispositive cases, however, the main rule is that parties remain liable for their own costs, unless there are special reasons to oblige one party to compensate the costs of the other party (OK 21:2). The custody and home of the child is generally considered as indispositive (KKO:2005:41) but in cases KKO:2003:104 and 105 on child alimony, the case was held as dispositive regarding the parent liable to pay alimonies but indispositive regarding the child as receiving the alimony. There is a recent precedent in which a mother with whom the children lived brought a case to get single custody of the children. The grounds included refusal by one of the children to meet father and allegations of threat and violence by the father. The claim was dismissed and joint custody confirmed. The mother had to pay legal costs € 13000 to father. KKO:2014:96. The decision reflects the strong presumption of joint custody in Finnish family law.

387. In KKO:2007:95 a case for discharging an executor of an estate was held indispositive but an order to compensate the costs to the executor was given.

388. In both types of cases, the party must present the claim for compensation and a bill of the costs to the court before the main hearing is concluded. The decision on the compensation of costs is included in the judgment (OK 21:14).

389. The court can make exceptions from the rule of full compensation in dispositive cases in the following cases:

390. First, if several claims are processed together and the parties both loose and win or a claim is accepted only in part, the compensation of the costs may be adjusted accordingly (OK 21:3; KKO:2007:96; KKO:2002:72; KKO:2002:71). An offer of settlement was taken into account when the court appreciated whether the claim was confirmed in part or in whole in KKO:2008:52.

391. Second, the right to compensation is adjusted if the party incurred unnecessary costs or an unnecessary lawsuit (KKO:2004:13). This rule can even be applied to the representative of a party or to an advocate (OK 21:4–5).

392. Third, if the case involved legal issues so uncertain and unclear that the losing party had a reasonable ground to sue, the court can decide that parties are partly or totally liable for their own costs (OK 21:8a; KKO:2002:89). This rule was first repealed during the 1993 reform. During the reform of civil procedure, insurance companies curtailed their compensation rules so that they no longer covered the costs of the opposite party and the costs of litigation increased and became prohibitive for litigation. The rule on non-compensation of the costs in cases of legal uncertainty was added again to the law in 1999. It seems, however, that it is applied more carefully than before the 1993 reform.

393. Fourth, in 1999 a possibility to adjust the compensation rules on the basis of equity, taking into account the nature of the case, the circumstances of the parties and the meaning of the case for the party, was also introduced (KKO:2004:23).

394. The claim for the compensation of costs when the parties have settled the main dispute is sometimes left for the court to decide. The Supreme Court sees no obstacle to such a procedure. It orders full compensation (KKO:1996:131) or partial compensation (KKO:1997:77) depending on the content of the settlement.

395. The costs to be compensated according to the above-mentioned rules must be reasonable and necessary (OK 21:1). The compensation of costs includes court fees, evidentiary costs, the advocate's fee and costs of the party for the preparation of the trial. In summary cases, the compensated costs are regulated by a decree of the ministry of justice (OK 21:8c; Decree of the Ministry of Justice on the Compensation of the Costs of the Opposite Party according to Ch. 21 § 8c of the Code of Procedure (1311/2001)). After the last amendment of the § 3 of this decree (425/2012) the costs are compensated according to the following table (debt capital). In individual cases, extra real costs can be charged as defined in the Degree. The compensation due in principle within one month after the verdict, and the interest for the compensation is regulated in detail (OK 21:8.2).

Table 2 Standard Costs in Summary Payment Claims

	Debt below EUR 300	*Debt EUR 300–1000*	*Debt over EUR 1000*
Normal case	50	80	110
Difficult case	80	120	160

Part VII. Evidence (2016)

Chapter 1. Burden of Proof

§1. Free Evaluation and Reception of Evidence

396. The Finnish law on evidence has been reformed in 1948 and in 2015. The basic principles of free evaluation and free reception of evidence were adopted in the reform of 1948 and sustained in 2015.[8] The reform in 2015 rewrote Chapter 17 of the Code of Procedure and amended several other laws (Law 732/2015, which enters into force on 1 January 2016). The reform was more focused on the criminal procedure and, thus, many of the regulations concerning civil procedure were changed only slightly. However, as Chapter 17 was rewritten, the paragraph numbering was changed. The references in this revised Part VII are to the new paragraphs.

397. The principles of free evaluation and free reception of evidence are believed to enhance the finding of material truth. The principle of material truth is valued in Finnish legal doctrine. Contemporary scholars make a distinction between the procedural truth, which is attained during trial, and the material truth, which should be approximated by the procedural truth. In civil procedure, however, the right of the parties to dispose of the claims and evidence compromises the role of material truth as a legal principle.

398. The principle of free evaluation of evidence is now explicitly stated in OK 17:1.2. The evaluation of evidence is left to the discretion of the court. As a rule, the law does not prescribe the evidentiary value of any piece of evidence.

399. There are some legal presumptions, that is, the law in some cases states that a circumstance may be presumed from certain facts. For example, the spouse is held as the father to a child born in wedlock (Paternity Act; *Isyyslaki* 11/2015). Another example are translations by authorized translators, which are held as valid unless otherwise proven (Law on authorized translators *Laki auktorisoiduista kääntäjistä;*

8. Actually, these principles already replaced the legal theory of evidence that was incorporated in the Code of 1734 in case law and practice (Pihlajamäki, 1997). The Code of 1734 operated with the concept of full proof and defined the evidentiary value of each testimony. As a rule, two witnesses accounted for the full proof. Of the principle Ervo 1997.

1231/2007 § 6). Opposing evidence can usually overturn these kinds of presumptions (OK 17:2,4).

400. In accordance with the principle of free evaluation of evidence, OK 17:6 specifically grants the court discretion to give the evidentiary value to the fact that a party fails to appear in court, to answer a question or to fulfil other requirements in the trial. Moreover, the court has a specific discretion to assess the reasonable amount of payment obligation, such as damages, when the quantity of the payment cannot be proved without unreasonable distress (OK 17:2.3).

401. The principle of free reception of evidence means that the law gives fairly few limitations to what kind of evidence may be presented (see Chapter 2 *infra*). The two principles go hand-in-hand. It is assumed that, using the powers of free evaluation of evidence, the court can divert any undue influence that biased evidence might have. Rules that exclude a certain type of evidence are seen as a threat to the clarification of the material truth. In practice, the courts have also a fairly permissive attitude towards reception of evidence. Evidence is seldom forestalled as irrelevant or excessive (see Chapter 2 *infra*).

§2. Basic Concepts

402. The facts in the case are divided into three categories: legal facts, evidentiary facts and auxiliary facts. Legal facts have an immediate relevance for the outcome of the case, that is, they are facts that immediately form the basis of the claim. The evidence in the case is always put forward to prove a legal fact.

403. It is often not possible to present evidence that directly proves a legal fact. Instead, the evidence proves a fact that supports the existence of a legal fact. Such facts are called evidentiary facts. The evidentiary facts either support or disprove a legal fact. For example, the authenticity of a signature can be an evidentiary fact that proves the promise (legal fact) based on a document.

404. Auxiliary facts do not by themselves say anything about the legal facts. They can only either increase or decrease the credibility or value of evidence about legal or evidentiary facts. Evidence about the circumstances in which a witness made her observations is an auxiliary fact.

405. A case may also be proven by circumstantial evidence. Circumstantial evidence is not based on direct observation of the legal facts but on a causal relationship between the evidence and the alleged legal fact. The evidentiary value of circumstantial evidence is often low but during the final evaluation of the evidence, several pieces of consistent circumstantial evidence can prove the case.

406. The evidentiary theme by which evidence is presented can be either a legal fact or an evidentiary fact. All evidence, however, must be presented to support one of the legal facts asserted by the party.

§3. The Burden of Proof

I. The Burden of Assertion

407. A party bears the burden to assert the legal facts, that is, the grounds for his claim (OK 17:2.1). This burden of assertion is generally applied to all legal facts relevant in a case. If the party declines to invoke a legal fact, it is not taken as a basis for the judgment.

408. The burden of assertion does not include the evidentiary facts which the court can assess, even if the party to whom such a fact is favourable has not specifically referred to it. Thus, auxiliary facts that can give credibility to a witness statement can be given weight even if they have come into sight in the evidence given by the opposing party.

409. The burden of assertion and burden of evidence generally fall to the same party but not always, as Virolainen pointed out. It is possible that neither party has the burden of assertion, for example in an indispositive case, but still the burden of proof for an uncertain fact has to be allocated to one of the parties (Virolainen, 1995a).

II. The Threshold of Evidence

410. The theory on the evaluation of evidence has been subject to considerable transformation in the legal doctrine during the past two decades and this development is reflected in the 2015 provision on burden of proof.[9] According to OK 17:2.2 in civil cases, a party has to present *credible evidence* of a (legal) fact before a judgment can be based on that fact.[10]

411. With the new law, the threshold of evidence in civil cases seems to be lower than before, when it was expressed as 'full proof' or as 'proven'. In doctrine, the threshold of 'preponderance of evidence' was rejected (see Lappalainen 2012 for example; in favour of it Saranpää 2010). Lappalainen, however, maintains that some types of cases must be decided on the preponderance of evidence and mentions as examples the best interest of the child in custody cases and the interpretation of a will (Lappalainen 2012, 695).

---

9. Timo Saranpää argued in his doctoral thesis for the threshold in civil cases to be put at the level of the preponderance of evidence (2010).
10. In older doctrine, Jouko Halila and Tauno Tirkkonen argued that the threshold of evidence was at the level of 'full proof' (Tirkkonen, 1949, 25; Tirkkonen, 1977; Halila, 1955). In addition, the personal conviction of the judge was underlined. The principle of 'the preponderance of evidence' according to which the party, who has proved his legal facts to be more probably true than the other party, wins, has not been accepted in the Finnish legal doctrine (Klami, Gräns & Sorvettula, 2000, 82). The former OK 17:2 covered both civil and criminal cases and, thus, it was possible to apply this expression in both kinds of cases.

412. It is to be seen how case law shall interpret the level credible evidence in the future.

413. In material law the threshold of evidence is sometimes specifically referred to as 'plausible' or 'probable' to indicate that the threshold is somewhat lower than usual or as 'obvious' or 'manifest' to indicate that the evidence should be particularly firm to prove the point. It is, however, questionable whether such expressions are used in a consistent way.

III. The Burden of Proof

414. The case must be decided in uncertainty by allocating the burden of proof to another party. Alternatively, as the threshold of evidence today is considered more flexible than before, the cases decided purely on the burden of proof seem to be fewer than before. On the other hand, since the threshold of evidence and the burden of proof are understood as bound together, the burden of proof is implicitly present in many cases. The court should clarify issues of burden of proof if they are unclear (KKO:2007:52).

415. The burden of proof is not allocated according to the formal position of the claimant and the defendant, but rather according to which of the parties asserted the legal facts in the case (OK 17:2.1-2). Thus, the position of the party in the material legal relationship gives guidance to the allocation of the burden of proof and the burden of proof is allocated differently depending on which legal facts each party invokes.

416. Sometimes the material law articulates the rule of burden of proof. For example, the Sale of Goods Act (*Kauppalaki* 355/1987) contains certain rules on the burden of proof articulated in such a way that a fact is presumed unless the seller or buyer proves otherwise (§§ 27, 40 and 57).

417. In the absence of a rule on the burden of proof, the following three general principles are applied. First, the burden of proof is to be allocated so that the functions of the material law on the issue are promoted or, at least, not hampered. Thus, the functioning of the credit market requires that the burden of proof of the payment of debt is allocated to the debtor.

418. Second, the party that asserts that something exceptional has happened or has been agreed upon has the burden of proof. Thus, normality is the norm. There may be some reason to be more cautious about this principle today than in the 1950s when it was articulated. In a multicultural society, normality is more difficult to establish and even what is considered normal for the majority of the people is not necessarily normal between the parties.

419. Third, the party, who has a better opportunity to ensure evidence about a fact, usually has the burden of proof for that fact.

§4. THE DISPOSITIVE PRINCIPLE

420. The dispositive principle is applied to the facts as well as to the claims. If the opposite party admits to a fact asserted by the other party, this fact is not under dispute and the court will take it as the basis of the judgment (OK 17:5.2). This right to agree on the facts includes the legal facts as well as the evidentiary facts. Only obviously false or impossible admissions are disregarded.

421. If the party later withdraws its admission, the court has discretion over the evidentiary value of the admission revoked (OK 17:5.3).

422. These rules do not apply to indispositive cases in which the court is not bound by the dispositions made by the parties (17:5.2-3).

423. In congruence with the dispositive principle, it is the responsibility of the parties to present the evidence. According to OK 17:7, the court can take the initiative to invite new evidence in indispositive cases. In dispositive cases, the court may on its own initiative only appoint an expert witness.

Chapter 2. Admissibility of Evidence

§1. Jura Novit Curia

424. Evidence is about facts. The facts to be proved can be of various arts. In addition to a fact in the individual case, facts of a more general character can also be proved. The rules of experience can be proved. Such rules can be deterministic natural laws, technical knowledge or statistical probabilities, which are proved by expert evidence or they can be rules of general experience.

425. There is no need to present evidence about the law. The principle *jura novit curia* means that the court knows the law ex officio (OK 17:4). It has to be noted, however, that the court can submit an interpretation of EU law to the European Court of Justice for a preliminary ruling in accordance with the conditions of TFEU 267.

426. The parties in commercial disputes sometimes present legal briefs on the legal issues in the case by the leading experts in the respective field of law. These briefs are part of the advocacy, not of evidence. However, a new rule explicitly allows such briefs (OK 17:4.1).

427. If the rules of international private law require that the law of another country be applied in the case, the information about this law can be acquired either by the parties or by the court (OK 17:4.2). The court acquires such information according to the European Convention on the Information on Foreign Law (ETS 62/1968) or through other channels. The court can exhort the party to present evidence on the foreign law. If no information on the foreign law is available, the court applies the Finnish law instead (OK 17:4.3). For example, in case KKO:1999:98, the Supreme Court held that the general information on the Spanish law on collateral presented by the bankruptcy estate party to the case was sufficient for the application in the dispute.

§2. Doctrine of Relevance

428. Not all facts need to be proved. According to the OK 17:5.1, facts that are generally known, so-called notorious facts, need not be proved. Likewise, facts that are known to the court ex officio, that is, facts that the court has been informed of in the course of its business, need not be proved.

429. The general principles, which guide what evidence the court can exclude, are set in OK 17:8 and 5:21.3. First, the court can exclude evidence that is irrelevant to the case (the principle of relevance; also in OK 17:48.6). Second, the court should exclude evidence of a fact that has already been proved (the principle of excessive evidence). Third, the court can exclude evidence if the fact can be proven in another manner with considerably less inconvenience or cost (the principle of efficiency). Fourth, the court should exclude evidence that can be replaced by more reliable evidence. Finally, the court should exclude evidence that is not possible to find, notwithstanding appropriate attempts, when the trial cannot be prolonged any more.

430. In the doctrine, it is argued that the principle of immediacy and the principle of best evidence require that the chain of evidence should be as short as possible.

431. These principles are applied with caution in practice. The courts historically had a fairly permissive attitude towards the principles of relevant and excessive evidence. The introduction of the preparatory stage of trial made it possible for the courts to take up these principles before the main hearing and, therefore, it is expected that these principles will be enforced more effectively in the future. Now, the more explicit rules in the new OK 17:8 give the courts a stronger position to control the expediency of the presentation of evidence.

432. It has to be noted, however, that the Finnish law on evidence has no rule on hearsay evidence. The principle of best evidence excludes hearsay evidence if direct evidence is possible to obtain. In other cases, the principle of relevance should guide the discretion of the courts.

§3. Inadmissibility of Illegally Obtained Evidence

433. In the framework of the 2015 reforms, a new rule on the inadmissibility of evidence that has been obtained through illegal means was added to the code (OK 17:25). Of course, evidence obtained by torture is forbidden (OK17:25.1). OK 17:25.3 sets out the general principles, which are applicable both to civil and criminal procedure. However, the provision has more relevance in the criminal procedure. The general principle guiding the discretion of the court is that evidence, even if obtained through illegal means, can be used as evidence as long as it does not risk fair trial. More specifically, the court should consider the nature of the case, how serious the violation of the rules was, how the credibility of the evidence was affected, the importance of the evidence for the outcome of the case and other circumstances.

§4. The Privilege Not to Testify

I. Relatives of a Party

434. Close relatives of a party have the privilege to refuse to testify (OK 17:17). The privilege extends to:

- a person who is or has been married to a party, including registered partnership;[11]
- a cohabiting partner;
- a person who is a direct ascendant or descendant of a party, including kinship based on adoption;
- a sibling of a party;
- a person who, based on partnership or family relationship, has a similar close relationship with a party.

435. The privilege is complete; the person does not need to testify or to give an affirmation (oath) at all. If the relative decides to testify, he is under the obligation to tell the truth and, in civil cases, to give an affirmation before giving testimony (OK 17:44). After agreeing to testify, a witness cannot choose which questions to answer or invoke the privilege only in cross-examination (KKO:1985 II 93; exception self-incrimination), nor cancel her agreement to testify. The privilege concerns only that party to whom the witness is closely related in case of joinder of parties (KKO:1960 II 92).

II. Self-Incrimination

436. The general principle that no one can be compelled to testify against oneself or to confess guilt is expressed in Article 14.3(g) of the International Covenant on Civil and Political Rights, which is part of the law in Finland. This general principle is specified concerning the trial in OK 17:18.1. It states that everyone is allowed to refuse to testify or to reveal a fact if one cannot do so without incriminating oneself. The witness has the same right if she would expose a close relative, as mentioned in OK 17:17, to such a risk.

III. Privilege of Trade Secrets and Mass Media

437. A person who is called as a witness can refuse to testify about professional or trade secrets (OK 17:19). This right is a privilege for the witness who may decide not to invoke the privilege and agree to testify. The privilege is not unconditional. The court may order the witness to testify, after considering the nature of the case, the importance of the evidence for the outcome of the case, the consequences of revealing the information and other circumstances.

438. The law does not restrict the privilege to persons who work in a company or are in a position of trust. In practice it concerns the entrepreneur, the legal representative of a company and employees. In addition, persons who have gained knowledge of trade secrets in other capacities, such as accountants, advisors or business partners, may invoke the privilege. Professional secrets can concern technical

11. Act on Registered Partnerships (*Laki rekisteröidystä parisuhteesta* 950/2001) § 8.

production methods, innovations and the like; trade secrets can concern marketing, pricing or other aspects of the business.

439. The regulation of the privilege can be in congruence with or collide with other regulations of confidentiality in commercial activity. Generally, the duty to keep professional and trade secrets is regulated in the Unfair Business Practices Act (*Laki sopimattomasta menettelystä elinkeinotoiminnassa* 1061/1978 § 4), but its specific scope is often based on contractual obligations between company and employee. In some cases, the confidentiality of customer or company files specifically is legally protected. Especially the relationship between confidentiality of bank secrecy (Act on Credit Institutions (*Laki luottolaitostoiminnasta* 610/2014) § 14)) and the right not to testify about professional and trade secrets has been subject to some controversy. The court's discretion regarding the privilege and the possibility to hold a hearing behind closed doors and to declare such documents confidential according to the Court Publicity Act (10 §), however, help to avoid problems.

440. The *confidentiality of the sources of information* of the media is protected by the Act on the Exercise of Freedom of Expression in Mass Media (*Laki sananvapauden käyttämisestä joukkoviestinnässä* 460/2003) § 16. According to that Act, the publisher, broadcaster and author are entitled to maintain the confidentiality of their source. The publisher and broadcaster also have a right not to reveal the author of an article or a message. According to the Code of Procedure 17:20, they have a corresponding privilege at the trial not to reveal a source.

441. The confidentiality of the sources is not enforced if the case concerns an offence punishable by imprisonment with six years or more, an attempt of or participation in such an offence, or information given in violation of a duty of secrecy, subject to punishment under a separate provision (OK 17:20.2).

442. The privilege of professional and trade secrets and the confidentiality of the source do not exempt the witness from appearing at the hearing or from giving an affirmation. It only gives a prerogative not to answer questions regarding such secrets.

IV. Confidentiality

443. No one can reveal confidential facts related to the protection of national security or of the rights and interests of Finland in relation to foreign countries (OK 17:10). This obligation to confidentiality concerns anyone who has knowledge of such secrets but, in practice, its subjects are civil servants. There is no mention of a waiver in the paragraph and it is unlikely that a need for a waiver would arise in a civil case. A case concerning such secrets is, in any case, handled behind closed doors.

444. The negotiations of the court before a judgment is given are confidential and no one may testify about them (OK 17:11.1; Court Publicity Act § 23; Act on the Publicity of Administrative Court Proceedings (*Laki oikeudenkäynnin julkisuudesta hallintotuomioistuimissa* 381/2007) § 15).

445. A mediator in mediation procedures that are regulated by specific laws[12] may not testify about the matter in mediation (OK 17:11.2-3). The court may order the mediator to testify, after considering the nature of the case, the importance of the evidence for the outcome of the case, the consequences of revealing the information and other circumstances. The mediator may also testify if the person, who is protected by confidentiality, agrees.

446. The right and duty to testify of the civil servants was totally reformed in 2015. The old provision referred only very generally to the confidentiality of the information, regulated elsewhere in legislation. The provision had not been amended since 1948, while the relevant laws and the broader context of the welfare state had, of course, been totally transformed during the past sixty-five years. Especially in the 2000s, the regulation of confidential information was subject to several legislative changes. Specifically, in 1999 a general Law on the publicity of public documents took the transparency of the public sector functions as its starting point (Publicity Act). However, the very same act regulates in detail which information the civil servants are obliged to keep confidential (especially Publicity Act § 24). In addition, the Act on the Rights of the Client of Social Services (*Laki sosiaalihuollon asiakkaan asemasta ja oikeuksista* 812/2000) now regulates the rights and duties of the social service authorities to give information at a trial in a detailed manner. Furthermore, when the Procedural Code's Chapter on evidence was enacted in 1948, the trials were public with very few exceptions. The public trial is still the general principle but the situations, in which a hearing and documents should be kept confidential, are regulated in a detailed manner (See General Introduction § 4, II). Thus, even if a witness is ordered to reveal confidential information at a trial, this information does not automatically become public.

447. According to the new OK 17:12, the main principle is that civil servants, employees of the public sector, persons in a position of trust in the public sector and others who are in a position, in which they have gained confidential information as mentioned in Publicity Act § 23, have a duty to testify. Publicity Act § 23.2 extends the regulation to those who have come into possession of confidential information through a commission or permission. The scope of persons thus defined is broader and better defined than before. As a consequence, also the scope of persons who can claim the privilege of certain information is also broader than before.

448. Thus, the new OK 17:12 regulates in detail the situations in which a civil servant may not testify. These situations are basically limited to situations, in which the party herself is not allowed to access the information according to Publicity Act

12. Act on mediation in civil matters and confirmation of settlements in general courts (*Laki riita-asioiden sovittelusta ja sovinnon* vahvistamisesta yleisissä tuomioistuimissa 394/2011) and Act on Conciliation in Criminal and Certain Civil Cases (*Laki rikosasioiden ja eräiden riita-asioiden sovittelusta* 1015/2005).

§ 11.2. Understandably, this is a very limited list and the purpose of some of the limitations is to protect one of the parties. In addition, the list includes certain preparatory stages in the actions of the public bodies. OK 17:12.2 lists other situations in which civil servants are not allowed to testify but these refer to criminal procedure.

449. The confidentiality of medical personnel is regulated in OK 17:14. In addition to medical doctors, it covers all professionals mentioned in the Act on Health Care Professionals (*Laki terveydenhuollon ammattihenkilöistä* 559/1994), such as psychologist, pharmacist, nurse, midwife, physiotherapist, dental/oral hygienist, optician or dental technician etc., students and assistants (OK 17:22.2).

450. In the new law of 2015, the confidential information has been defined as information about health, sensitive facts and secrets of an individual and her family. However, the person, who is protected by confidentiality, may agree to testimony.

451. The law of 2015 makes a distinction between a trial lawyer and other counsel regarding confidentiality (OK 17:13). Trial lawyers, their assistants and interpreters have an unconditional obligation not to testify when performing their duties during a trial or in the preparations for a trial or when counselling for instigating or avoiding a trial. The privilege is unconditional but the client may give permission to testify.

452. An attorney, a public attorney and a licensed lawyer (including assistants) have a wider privilege that encompasses their entire mandate, even if it does not have any connection to a (prospective) trial. This privilege covers the secrets of an individual and a family, as well as professional and trade secrets. The court may order the attorney to testify, after considering the nature of the case, the importance of the evidence for the outcome of the case, the consequences of revealing the information and other circumstances, if especially weighty reasons require that.

453. The duty to confidentiality of *a priest* is regulated in the Church Law for the evangelical church, to which the majority of the population belongs. Also, the confidentiality in the orthodox Christian church is regulated in a specific law. The confidentiality covers besides priests also deacons and parish lectors who may give pastoral counselling. The confidentiality is unconditional also at trial. The law of 2015 extends the confidentiality to other registered religious communities, regulated in the Freedom of Religion Act (*Uskonnonvapauslaki* 453/2003).

Chapter 3. Administration of Evidence

§1. Documentary Evidence

454. The rules on documentary evidence are in OK 17:9, 17:38-40. The concept of document covers basically all written evidence. Besides paper, a document can also be available in an electronic format. The documents in question can be either of a public or private nature (KKO:2011:27). The rules in Chapter 17 of Code of Procedure do not make a difference between public and private documents.

455. As a new principle, a copy of a document is sufficient, unless the court orders that the original has to be presented.

456. As a starting point, everyone in possession of a document that may have evidentiary value, can be ordered to bring it to the court (OK 17:9). This duty covers both the opposing party as well as any third parties. However, a person who has a privilege, either a duty or a right not to testify, may also decline to present the document to the court (OK 17:9.2). However, if only part of the document concerns such confidential issues, the obligation to present the document to the court remains. In such case, the confidential parts of the document are covered or otherwise hidden (OK 17:38.2).

457. As a basic rule, the parties attach the documentary evidence in their applications for the summons or their party statements. At the main hearing, the documentary evidence is alleged, either during the party statements or at the beginning of the presentation of the evidence. The documents are sometimes read aloud, but usually it suffices to refer to the relevant content of the document.

458. The party, when asked during the preparation of the trial, has a duty to inform the court and the opposite party whether the party is in possession of a certain document (OK 5:20).

459. If the party does not have possession of the document and the person who does will not voluntarily give it to the court, the party can request the court to give an order to relinquish the document.

460. In principle, the document has to be identified before the court can give an order to deliver it. The identification has to be so clear that the enforcement authorities can enforce the order of the court if it is not fulfilled voluntarily. For example, a general order including documents that have relevance in the case has not been accepted (discovery). It is not required, however, that the identification singles out just one document. Leppänen argued that the identification should include the type of the document, the evidentiary theme and the date of the document (1998a, p. 236–238).

461. The person in possession of the document has the right to be heard before an order to deliver a document is given (OK 17:40.2). Usually, the person is asked to deliver his/her opinion in a written procedure but also a hearing may be organized. The court may set a threat of a payment to guarantee that the order to present the document is obeyed. The court may also order the enforcement agent to fetch the document.

§2. Witnesses

I. Competence to Appear as a Witness

462. In principle, anyone who is not a party can appear as a witness.

463. If a child under the age of 15 or a mentally handicapped person is named as a witness, the court will specifically consider whether the hearing is necessary and can be made without causing harm to this witness (OK 17:27; 17:30). In addition, the testimony must be essential for the clarification of the matter. A testimony of such a person can be heard in a special hearing outside the main hearing (OK 17:56) or through a video link in the main hearing (OK 17:52.1 point 5). Such a person will not give an affirmation of truth. In OK 17:24.3 is regulated the use of videos or other recordings made during crime investigation. Even if the regulations refer to criminal procedure, the use of such recordings should be allowed also in civil procedure if the witness is under 15 or mentally impaired.

464. The parties are not heard as witnesses but they can be heard for the purpose of gathering evidence (see § 3 *infra*). The legal representatives of the parties, such as a legal custodian or an executive director and the members of the executive board of a company or of an association, cannot be heard as witnesses (KKO:1986 II 145; KKO:1991:149). A person, who was a party or a legal representative earlier, can be heard as a witness. The decision is made with regard to the situation at the time of the hearing (KKO:1992:25).

II. Duty to Appear as a Witness

465. To appear as a witness is considered the duty of each person (OK 17:9). Only the President of the Republic cannot be called as a witness (OK 17:32).

466. A person assumed to know something that can be of relevance as evidence in the case can be compelled to appear as a witness at the trial. If the witness is present at the hearing, he or she may be heard immediately. Normally, the court issues the summons to appear as a witness during the preparation of the trial. The summons includes a notice that the sanction for failure to appear is a fine. The court may also let the party call the witness (OK 17:41).

467. If a witness, who has been subpoenaed, fails to appear in court, he or she will be fined and can be brought to court (OK 17:62). The witness, ordered to be brought to court, can be taken into custody five days before the hearing and will be liable for the costs so incurred. According to OK 12:28, no sanctions are imposed if the witness has a valid excuse.

468. In the framework of the 2015 reform, the religious oath was abolished. Now, the witness gives an affirmation of truth and has the duty to truthfully tell everything he or she knows about the case. If the witness refuses to give the affirmation or to answer questions without a valid reason, the Court can compel the witness to testify by ordering a fine or imprisonment up to six months (OK 17:63).

469. The wording of the affirmation is as follows: 'I, [insert name], do promise and swear on my honour and conscience that I shall testify and state the whole truth in this case, without concealing it, adding to it or altering it.' Perjury is sanctioned according to Criminal Code 15:1.

III. Hearing the Witness

470. The witnesses are heard at the main hearing after the opening statements of the parties, presentation of the documentary evidence and the hearing of the parties about the facts.

471. The witness gives the testimony orally. The main rule is that affidavits or other written testimonies are not allowed (OK 17:24; for exceptions see below § 5). This prohibition includes all private written statements drawn up for the purpose of a pending or imminent trial. However, the court has the power to admit a written statement by a witness if (1) both parties in a dispositive case agree to it, (2) a defendant, who disputes a written promissory note or similar proof of a payment obligation, gives to court a statement supporting her claim, or (3) another legal provision allows such a statement to be used as evidence.

472. In criminal procedures, the investigation protocols can be invoked if the witness retracts her statement in the protocol or cannot be reached (OK 17:24.2 and 17:47.2). There is no similar rule for the civil procedure but such a previous statement could be accepted as documentary evidence when the witness gives a different statement in court, using an analogous interpretation. In any case, documentary evidence can be invoked during the interrogation to point out differences in the testimony as compared to the document in question.

473. The witness is not present at the hearing before testifying (OK 17:60.2). When the witness is called in, the presiding judge first checks the identity of the witness. If needed, the witness will be asked if there is any reason that could entitle the witness to refuse to testify or prevent to give an affirmation. If the witness is entitled not to testify, the court notes that.

474. The court can also inquire about circumstances that could affect the credibility of the witness. At this point, the witness is usually asked about formal ties to the parties, such as kinship (even if it does not entitle a refusal), employment or a managerial position that could affect credibility.

475. Normally, the witnesses of the claimant are heard first and then the witnesses of the defendant (about the hearing Haapasalo, Kiesiläinen & Niemi-Kiesiläinen 2000). It is also possible to hear the witnesses for each evidentiary theme one after another. Two witnesses can be heard against each other, that is, at the same time but this rarely happens (OK 17:51).

476. The examination of the witness is divided into examination-in-chief, cross-examination and re-examination. First, the party who has named the witness examines her. The purpose of the examination-in-chief is to give the witness an opportunity to give an uninterrupted and spontaneous narrative of the evidentiary theme. It is not uncommon for a judge to first request the witness to give a narrative in order to achieve this aim. Especially if the party has no counsel or if both parties have named the witness, the court has a more active role even in the further examination of the witness (OK 17:48).

477. After the narrative, the counsel of the party who has named the witness examines the witness. Often the spontaneous narrative is short and the counsel helps the witness with questions. The questions in the examination-in-chief should be aimed at helping a narrative. Leading questions are explicitly forbidden (OK 17:48.6).

478. After the examination-in-chief, the opposite party has a right to cross-examination. Cross-examination is, in principle, restricted to the evidentiary theme given by the party that named the witness. In practice, however, questions about other themes are also allowed if other evidence presented at the trial gives reason for such questions. In cross-examination, leading questions are allowed to test the credibility of the witness.

479. In re-examination, the party who has named the witness can ask her questions. Then the other party and the members of the court may ask questions. Leading questions are allowed in the re-examination to test the reliability of the witness.

480. There are no rules in the examination of a hostile witness, that is, a witness who refuses to testify or who gives a statement in contradiction with what the witness has said before the trial. In those cases, the party who named the witness can retract from a further hearing. In that case, the opposite party names the witness.

481. A party can be expelled from the courtroom during the examination of a witness in exceptional situations but his counsel is of course present. The party can be expelled when necessary for the protection of the witness or a close relative, if the witness does not disclose what she knows in the presence of the party or if the party disturbs the witness (OK 17:51). This procedure is almost never used in civil cases but, for example, in a dispute over the custody of children the provision can have a preventive effect on an aggressive party.

482. The examination of a witness can be carried out through a video conference or a similar solution (1) if the witness cannot appear in court due to illness or another reason, (2) if the appearance causes considerable costs or inconvenience, (3) if the credibility of the witness can be evaluated on the basis of the video link, (4) if the witness of a close relative needs to be protected or (5) if the witness is younger than 15 or mentally impaired (OK 17:52). During the videoconference, the parties are allowed to ask the witness questions.

483. The witness can be even heard by telephone in situation 1–3 above.

484. The examination of the witness is recorded and the recording is stored for six months after the decision in the respective court or until the case is finally decided (OK 22:6 and 22:10). The recording normally is not transcribed (OK 22:9).

§3. Party Testimony

485. According to Finnish law, neither the parties nor their legal representatives are heard as witnesses. Nevertheless, the parties are heard at the trial to clarify facts and their statements are given evidentiary value. The rules on a party hearing are stated in Chapter 17 of the Code of Procedure. In 1993, the rules on party testimony were reformed in order to shape the hearing of a party about the facts and to make a clear distinction between the presentation of the claims and the pleadings of the party and the party testimony about the facts. After the reform, the parties present their claims and counterclaims and give their grounds in the opening discussion at the main hearing. After the opening discussion, the evidence is presented, usually starting with the hearing of the parties about the facts.

486. The option to hear parties under an affirmation of truth was abolished in 2015. This option was practically never used.

487. Thus, the parties are heard freely with the purpose of clarifying the matter. In accordance with the principle of free evaluation of evidence, the court assesses the evidentiary value of the party testimony.

488. The court has the power to compel the party to attend the trial and, if the party does not appear, he can be fined and brought to court. Unlike a witness, the party is not obliged to give a testimony or to answer questions or to give an oath. If the party declines to answer questions or come forward with information, the court has the discretion to assess what evidentiary meaning and value this has (OK 17:6).

489. There has been an extensive discussion in the doctrine about the duties of the party when heard freely. Undoubtedly, the party must speak truthfully about the facts of the case or when answering the questions (OK 14:1; OK 17:26). Even if the party cannot be punished for perjury, the doctrine holds that the party can be punished for fraud if false information given during the trial causes economic loss to the other party or a third person (KKO:1991:109). The disputed issue is whether a party has an obligation to come forward with all the information concerning the facts of the case. It is argued that after the 1993 reform, the party's obligation to give information about relevant facts has become stronger (Lappalainen 2012).

490. The examination of a party takes place in the same order as the examination of a witness (OK 17:48).

§4. Expert Evidence

491. While the witness is heard about the facts in the case, the expert testifies about the rules of experience that are relevant for the case and gives his opinion on the conclusions that can be drawn from the facts on the basis of his expertise. The difference between a witness and an expert is not always clear-cut. If the witness has special expertise in the area, she will nevertheless be heard as a witness if she has made immediate observations of the object.

492. Medical doctors are the most commonly relied upon experts in the Finnish courtrooms. If the doctor has examined or operated on the patient, he or she is usually heard as a witness, albeit as an expert witness. If the doctor gives his or her statement on the basis of the documents, he or she is heard as an expert. Evidently, the situation is somewhat blurred if the examination takes place for the sole purpose of trial, for example, when a psychiatrist examines the patient to testify about the consequences of an accident.

493. After the 2015 reform, an expert can be appointed by a party or the court (OK 17:7).[13] This rule confirms the earlier practice that the parties rely on expert witnesses and appoint them. However, the earlier rules on expert testimony only applied to court appointed experts. Since 2015, the same rules apply to party appointed experts as court appointed experts.

494. The expert must be honest and known for his/her qualifications in the area (OK 17:35). The expert must be impartial and cannot have any relationship with a party that would impair his/her impartiality (OK 17:36).

495. Unlike a witness, the expert gives his/her statement in writing (OK 17:36). If the Court deems it necessary, the expert is heard at the main hearing (OK 17:37). The expert gives an affirmation before he/she is heard (OK 17:45).

496. The hearing of an expert at the trial follows the same rules as the hearing of a witness (OK 17:48-49).

13. Before the reform, the law stated that an expert is one appointed by the court (OK 17:44 repealed). If a party relied on an expert, the person was heard as a witness (OK 17:55 repealed).

497. In a civil case, the parties are liable to compensate the expert's expenses and to pay the expert's fee. If only one of the parties requested the appointment of the expert, that party will be liable for the compensation (OK 17:66). If the expert holds an office with a public authority and the expert testimony is part of the expert's job, compensation is paid only in special cases. If a party relies upon an expert witness, this party is first liable to cover the expert's expenses and fee and the court decides at the end of the trial which party is liable for the expenses according to the Chapter 21 of Code of Procedure.

§5. Affidavits

498. The main rule is that affidavits or other written testimonies are not allowed (OK 17:24). This prohibition includes private written statements drawn up for the purpose of a pending or imminent trial. However, the court has the power to admit a written statement by a witness if (1) both parties in a dispositive case agree to it; (2) a defendant, who disputes a written promissory note or similar proof of a payment obligation, renders a statement supporting his/her claim, or (3) a legal provision allows such a statement to be used as evidence.

§6. Inspection On-Site

499. An object can be presented to the court as evidence. The court can give an order to deliver such an object in the same procedure as is followed concerning an order to deliver a document.

Everyone in the possession of an object that can be assumed to have significance as evidence is obliged to deliver it to the court, if it can be done without undue inconvenience (OK 17:40). If the person, who is in possession of an object requested as evidence, would have the privilege to refuse to testify according to OK 17:9.2, this person is exempted from the duty to deliver the object as evidence.

500. The court can order an inspection on-site if the matter of the dispute concerns real estate or a place or if an object cannot be brought to court (OK 17:9.1 and 17:40). An inspection on-site can be arranged before the main hearing. It is also possible that the court makes a visit on-site during the main hearing. The inspection on-site is usually made with the same members of the court that hear the case at the main hearing. At the preparatory stage, however, a judge can make the inspection alone even if the case is heard in a panel (OK 2:5.1). The court must give the person who is in charge of the place or object of inspection a chance to be heard before the decision to visit the place is made (OK 17:40.1). Everyone has the duty to allow an inspection to be made, in the same manner as everyone has the duty to appear as a witness. This duty can be backed with a threat of a pecuniary sanction. Even the police may be ordered to help to secure an inspection on-site. The parties are notified of the time of the inspection on-site.

Part VIII. Particular Procedures

Chapter 1. Summary Proceedings

501. Summary proceedings for the recovery of a payment obligation as a separate procedure either in the district courts (*maksamismääräys*) or in the enforcement authorities (*lainhaku*) were abolished during the 1993 reform of civil procedure. After the reform, the recovery of simple payment obligations is handled by the district courts according to a simplified civil procedure (summary proceeding; see Ervo 2001). The European payment order and the European small claims procedure can be filed at the District Court of Helsinki (Laws 753/2008 and 754/2008).

502. The claim in a summary proceeding must be either:

- a monetary payment obligation of a specified amount; or
- restitution of a specified object; or
- eviction (OK 5:3).

503. The claimant must notify the court that he assumes that the claim will not be contested.

504. Institutional creditors, such as banks and debt collection agencies, file their applications for summary proceedings electronically. The Ministry of Justice authorizes the users of electronic documents in the proceedings. All documents, with the exception of serving a summons, can also be sent electronically to such users.

505. The court issues summons, which is then served to the defendant who is given a deadline of usually two weeks to answer in writing. The defendant can contest the claim but is required to state the grounds on which the claim is contested. In addition, the defendant must notify the court of what evidence will be presented in the case. If the defendant states relevant grounds for the contestation, the claim will be processed as an ordinary civil case from then on.

506. In the summons, the defendant is exhorted to respond and is notified that if she fails to do so, the case can be concluded with a default judgment.

507. The court clerks and secretaries who have the necessary training usually process the summary proceedings in the district court. If the claim is complicated, it should be referred to a judge (The District Court Act § 19).

508. The default judgment is, in principle, based on formal grounds. Either the defendant failed to respond to the summons or the defendant objected to the claim but failed to state such grounds for the objection that can be relevant to the case. The court does, however, make a summary examination of the claim. If the claim is manifestly unfounded, the court will not give a default judgment.

509. The legal costs in summary proceedings are specifically regulated. The court must approximate the legal costs in summary proceedings ex officio (OK 21:8c) and according to a scale confirmed by the Ministry of Justice.

510. The default judgment can immediately be enforced. The defendant can, however, apply for the reopening of a case in the district court within thirty days after being served the default judgment (OK 12:15–17). Usually the default judgment is served to the defendant when the plaintiff applies its enforcement with the execution officer. The reopening of a case does not automatically stop the enforcement of the default judgment, but the court can, after an application from the debtor, suspend the enforcement.

511. The claimant, whose application for a default judgment was not accepted, can appeal to the appeal court. Also, the judgment given after the reopening of the case can be appealed.

Chapter 2. Family Law Cases

512. Several matters of a non-contentious nature are filed by application (see Part III, Chapter 1, § 1). This group of cases is heterogeneous but the most important application matters are family law cases, such as divorce, custody of children and the nomination of a custodian to an adult. There were circa 40,000 application matters in the district courts in 2013 (See Marriage Act § 28, Child Custody Act § 14.1, Guardianship Services Act § 69).

513. If an application matter is disputed, the court can decide that the case is handled according to the ordinary civil procedural rules.

514. Family law is partly indispositive by nature, especially when it concerns the best interest of the child. Therefore, the rules that govern an indispositive case are followed when an indispositive claim is presented and handled. According to the specific rules on quorum in family law cases, the court consists either of the judge alone or a panel of three judges.

515. Since divorce is granted on formal grounds after a six-month reconsideration period or after two years of separation, the divorce itself is seldom disputed. Other claims concerning the custody of children or the division of property filed together with the divorce can be disputed. Such disputed claims can be handled according to the normal rules of civil procedure.

Chapter 3. Court Matters and *Jurisdictio Voluntaria*

516. The court makes various decisions on procedural issues. They are usually decided upon as side issues in ordinary civil proceedings but they can also be filed as separate application matters. One specific example is the submission of a decision of the legal aid office to the court (Legal Aid Act § 24). Another example is the challenge of the arbitrator's award according to the Arbitration Act § 47.

517. These matters are processed according to Chapter 8 of the Code of Procedure.

Chapter 4. Class Actions

518. The Act on Class Actions was enacted in 2007 after a long preparation and several committee reports. It covers only consumer law matters, excluding however disputes on security markets. As of today, not one single class action has been filed in the Finnish courts.

519. A class action could only be filed by the Consumer Ombudsman (§ 4). When an action is filed, the plaintiff must notify potential class members about the case before the summons are given. The notification is made by post or email and possibly also by an ad in the newspapers. Then the potential class members have a possibility to opt-in. After the deadline for opt-in has passed, the plaintiff prepares the final application for summons. Opt-in is possible also later during the preparatory stage (§ 12). The court must in the judgment specify, which group members the judgment covers (§ 16). The group members are not liable for legal costs; these are borne by the Consumer Ombudsman/the State or the defendant according to the normal rules in OK Chapter 21 (§ 17).

Chapter 5. Insolvency Proceedings

520. There are three insolvency proceedings: bankruptcy, business reorganization and debt adjustment for private individuals. These are separate proceedings, regulated in three different laws, the Bankruptcy Act (*Konkurssilaki* 120/2004), Restructuring of Enterprises Act and the Act on the Adjustment of the Debts of a Private Individual (*Laki yksityishenkilön velkajärjestelystä* 57/1993). The bankruptcy proceedings aim at the liquidation of the debtor's business. The reorganization aims to the acceptance of a business reorganization and debt-rescheduling plan. In the debt adjustment, the aim is the rehabilitation of the economy of a private individual through a partial payment of debts according to a three-year payment plan and a relief from the rest of the debt burden.

521. The ground for each of these insolvency proceedings is insolvency of the debtor. For the debt adjustment of individuals, the insolvency must be qualified, that is, the debtor has no prospect of paying the debts within several years. An application for bankruptcy or reorganization can be made both by the debtor and by the creditors. Only the debtor can file for debt adjustment. The district court where the debtor as a natural person has the general venue has competence over bankruptcy and debt adjustment proceedings (BA 7:2, Debt Adjustment Act § 49.3). The competence for reorganization is vested in fourteen district courts mentioned in Restructuring of Enterprises Act § 67. The district court where a legal person has his main place of administration has competence over the bankruptcy and reorganization proceedings of the legal persons.

522. Each of the insolvency acts includes specific rules on procedure. See especially the Bankruptcy Act, Chapter 7, the Restructuring of Enterprises Act, Chapter 10 and the Debt Adjustment Act, Chapter 8. In the absence of such specific rules, the procedural rules for application matters in Chapter 8 of the Code of Procedure are followed (Bankruptcy Act 7:4.2, Reorganization Act § 68 and Debt Adjustment Act § 49.1).

Part IX. Seizure for Security and Enforcement of Judgments

Chapter 1. Seizure for Security

§1. PROCEEDINGS

523. The general regulations on provisional remedies (injunctions) in civil procedure are in Chapter 7 of the Code of Procedure with important complementary rules in Chapter 8 of the Enforcement Code. Both chapters were totally reformed in 1993 (1065/1991 and 1066/1991).

524. The rules on the enforcement of civil judgments are also followed when provisional measures concerning taxes and other public fees are ordered. Complementary regulations are, however, found in the Act of Provisional Measures for Taxes (*Laki verojen ja maksujen perimisen* turvaamisesta 395/1973) and the Enforcement of Taxes and Payments Act (*Laki verojen ja maksujen täytäntöönpanosta* 706/2007).

525. Also, a number of additional provisions are found in special laws, such as the Bankruptcy Act (4:8-9) and the Maritime Law. According to Chapter 4 of the Maritime Law, provisional measures in rem can be used to arrest a ship on the basis of certain claims caused by the use of the ship. The procedures are regulated in the Code of Procedure.

526. According to the Marriage Act the court can, in connection with the divorce, give temporary orders about alimony, custody of children and other measures (The Marriage Act § 31, as amended by law 411/1987; The Act on the Enforcement of a Custody Decision (*Laki lapsen huoltoa ja tapaamisoikeutta koskevan päätöksen täytäntöönpanosta* 619/1996).

527. In a criminal procedure, provisional seizure can be obtained to secure a civil claim to damages based on the criminal act (The Coercive Measures Act (*Pakkokeinolaki* 806/2011) Chapter 6). Seizure to secure evidence for a criminal trial is also regulated by this law.

528. According to the Freedom of Expression Act § 18, an injunction to stop the distribution of a network message, when the publication evidently means a criminal offence, can be stopped by the district court. A tort action must be brought within three months in court.

529. Certain injunction types of provisional measures are regulated in administrative law and procedures. Examples are legislation protecting the objects of national cultural heritage (Act on Restrictions to the Export of Cultural Goods (*Laki kulttuuriesineiden maastaviennin rajoittamisesta* 115/1999) and Act on the Return of Cultural Objects Unlawfully Removed from the Territory of the European Economic Area (*Laki Euroopan talousalueen valtion alueelta laittomasti vietyjen kulttuuriesineiden palauttamisesta* 1276/1994).

530. The two main conditions for the order of a provisional remedy in civil procedure are:

(a) the petitioner has brought prima facie evidence (probable cause) to support the right he alleges; and
(b) in the eyes of the judge, there is a presumable immediate risk for sabotage or infringement of the petitioner's right.

531. According to Chapter 7:1–3 of the Code of Procedure, provisional remedies are available for the preservation of the following claims:

(a) monetary claims on a civil liability, due under or without a contract, for example a tort; also taxes and fees under public law qualify (though with some special restrictive rules);
(b) claims for the possession of goods or realty, whether based on or derived from ownership or a lesser title. The object can be a corporeal good or an immaterial/intangible object (e.g., a trademark) or a document (e.g., a share certificate);
(c) claims for an order to:
    (i) prohibit the deed or action of the opposing party, under threat of a fine;
    (ii) order the opposing party to do something, under threat of a fine;
    (iii) empower the petitioner to do something or to have something done;
    (iv) order that property of the opposing party be placed under the administration and care of a trustee; or
    (v) order other measures necessary for securing the right of the petitioner to be undertaken.

532. It is possible to order a provisional remedy in most types of matters of real estate or movables or in any matter of law of contract or law of torts. The same applies to almost any kind of economical and commercial disputes, including professional sports. On the contrary, a great part of the disputes in the fields of labour and social security are excluded. Provisional protection of a person's privacy, integrity, and reputation should be available (see point (c) *supra*). However, it is not quite clear how the requirement of an action on the main claim is possible according to Finnish law. The legal costs for the winning party in the remedy proceedings cannot be included in the protective sphere of the remedy.

533. There is a risk of prejudice for the petitioner's right before and during the time of the procedure on the merits. Whether such a risk of abuse, concealment, dispossession, consumption, dissipation, waste, illegal nuisance or fraud can be assumed to exist in the petitioner's case depends on the discretion of the judge. In money claims, the burden of proof for the petitioner concerning the prognosis of the risk is low (KKO:1994:132 and KKO:1994:133).

534. When deciding on the issue of a prohibition or an order referred to in (c) *supra*, the court sees to it that the opposing party does not suffer undue inconvenience in comparison with the benefit to be secured (OK 7:3.2). The burden of proof for the presumed risk is higher than in points (a) and bb) above and related to the disputed benefit that the applicant would enjoy before the judgment (KKO:1998:143 and KKO:2003:118).

535. The law does not dispose the content of the provisional remedy *a priori*. On the contrary, the law gives the judge a wide discretion to dispose according to the circumstances (especially OK 7:3). As to money claims, the content of the remedy is usually an attachment or seizure of (a part of) the defendant's property to an amount sufficient to cover the claimed sum.

536. This flexibility in forms of protection is of great practical importance in cases where the remedy is to preserve another right than a money claim. In other types of rights, the remedy can have prohibitory and/or mandatory elements, mostly for a preventive or conservative purpose. The judge can set a fine as a penalty for negligence of an injunction order. One possibility is to order the placement of the disputed property under the temporary managerial administration of a trustee.

537. The provisional measures are granted by the district court where the proceedings are presided over by a single judge. When the Market Court has jurisdiction over the main action, it also decides on the injunctions (OK 7:4; 119/2013)

538. Provisional protection can be applied both before the claim on the merits is filed (pre-trial) and during the trial (pendente lite). At the initial stage, the provisional protection can be ordered as a temporary injunction in urgent cases. Such temporary injunction is ordered without hearing the defendant and only when an application for the provisional protection is made simultaneously (OK 7:5). After a temporary injunction is granted, the defendant is summoned as soon as the urgent purpose of such an interimistic remedy is achieved. The defendant is then entitled to full use of his constitutional right to be heard. The claims for provisional measures are usually decided in written proceedings. The parties have, however, a right to a hearing, but this right is not often invoked.

539. As a rule with very few exceptions, the remedy is enforceable. The ways to enforce remedy orders are, in general, the same as those adopted with the judgments on the merits. The most important difference is, of course, that the enforcement authority usually retains the property or documents seized during the main trial.

540. To enforce the provisional remedy, the petitioner has to file a request with the execution officer. In addition, the petitioner has to lodge a security in favour of the defendant for the eventual damage or loss the defendant may suffer if the remedy is later found to be unjustified (UK 8:2). The security is given to an execution officer who decides on the type (most often a bank guarantee or sometimes a collateral item or a real estate mortgage) and value of acceptable security and who receives it for retention.

541. The judge has the power to grant relief to the plaintiff from the obligation to deposit a security as a condition of enforcement of provisional remedies (OK 7:7). It can be granted if the plaintiff is indigent and his right is highly probable. This relief is only seldom granted in practice.

542. The defendant can prevent or revoke the enforcement of injunctions for the protection of money claims by lodging a sufficient ward-off security with the execution officer (UK 8:3). In non-money remedies, the petitioner may accept a security or the execution officer may consider, on a case-by-case basis, that a ward-off security offered by the defendant is adequate and satisfactory.

§2. Judicial Review

543. The provisional remedies ultimately depend on the proceedings on the merits. If proceedings on merits are not pending when the provisional remedy is granted, the plaintiff is obliged to start a proceeding on the merits within one month from the decision (OK 7:6). This time limit cannot be prolonged. The claimant is obliged to bring evidence of the commencement of the proceedings on merits to the enforcement official in order to keep the provisional remedy in force.

544. The most common proceedings on the merits are civil actions in the first instance court, which is the same court that has jurisdiction for provisional measures. In practice, a filing for a civil law suit is often accompanied by a simultaneous claim for provisional protection. As a main rule, the same judge can preside over both the provisional remedy proceedings and the ordinary trial on the merits.

545. The proceedings on the merit can, however, be any other proceedings that lead to an enforceable decision. For example, proceedings in an arbitration tribunal, an administrative court, in a special court or in a foreign court and in criminal proceedings qualify for proceedings on the merits.

546. During the proceedings on the merits, the court can, on demand of the defendant, revoke the provisional remedy if the judge finds that the grounds for the remedy no longer exist (e.g., there is no longer any risk of sabotage on the part of the defendant). Also, if the final judgment on the merits is negative for the petitioner, the judge must decide whether the remedy will lose its effects immediately or whether the defendant will have to wait until the judgment has become res judicata.

547. The unsatisfied party can appeal against the judge's final ex audita decision to order or to refuse a provisional remedy (OK 7:14). As to interim remedies *(ex inaudita)*, no appeal is allowed, due to their brief duration. In addition, when a decision on merits is appealed, the provisional remedies can be challenged as well. In both cases, an appeal is lodged in the Court of Appeal.

548. The suspension of the enforcement of the provisional remedy order is, in principle, obtainable as soon as the defendant has lodged an appeal. Whether this temporary suspension request is approved, depends on an *in casu* discretion of the justices, as they prima facie appraise the chances of the appeal to be approved, in consideration of the extent of the inconvenience likely to be suffered on each side. On the other hand, if a petitioner, whose petition was refused by the first instance judge, lodges the appeal, there is a possibility for the Court of Appeal to immediately order a temporary provisional remedy. This alteration in favour of the petitioner can happen if the Court of Appeal, in its prima facie survey of the petitioner's appeal documents, finds the position taken by the first instance judge incorrect or doubtful, with due consideration of the extent of the inconvenience likely to be suffered on each side.

549. The most important safeguard for the defendant is that the claimant is liable for any damage or losses that the provisional measure caused if the outcome of the final judgment on the merits indicates (expressly or indirectly) that the remedy was unjustified. This liability is claimed in a separate trial that the defendant must initiate within one year from the removal of the remedy (OK 7:12). The liability of the petitioner is strict, that is it is irrespective of the petitioners fault or negligence (KKO:1998:59 and 1998:96). For example, in case KKO:1998:59 the provisional measure was enforced by taking the document that entitled the defendant to the possession of his home. Thus, the defendant was not able to sell her home and had to turn down a favourable offer. The claimant, a bank, was ordered to compensate the loss.

Chapter 2. Enforcement of Judgments

§1. Enforcement of Domestic Judgments

I. Proceedings

550. The Execution Act, originally enacted in 1895, was under a gradual reform process during the 1990s and 2000s. Partial reforms were consolidated to a new Enforcement Code that entered into force 1 January 2008.[14]

551. The enforcement authorities are state authorities. The central enforcement authority is located in the city of Turku, under the Ministry of Justice. Regional enforcement agencies are also state authorities. There are twenty-one regional enforcement agencies (Degree of the Government on regional enforcement areas 865/2007).

552. The head of the enforcement agency (*kihlakunnanvouti*) is the regional head execution officer who has competence to make the most important decisions concerning the enforcement procedure. The execution officers (*ulosottomies)* do the practical enforcement work. The execution officer has a central role in the enforcement.

553. The head execution officer has the competence to make legal decisions concerning the procedure and the rights of the parties in the enforcement process. He can delegate decision-making powers to other execution officers (UK 1:7–8). Their decisions can be appealed to fourteen designated district courts (UK 11:2.2). The decisions of the district courts can be appealed to the Courts of Appeal and further to the Supreme Court.

554. Several private companies are active in the debt collection sector. Their operations are regulated in the Debt Collection Law (*Laki saatavien perinnästä* 513/1999) and are under the surveillance of the Consumer Ombudsman who can request an injunction against unlawful collection measures in the market court (§§ 12–14). The law refers generally to the good debt collection practices that the debt collection agencies are obliged to follow. They have no right to take coercive measures against the debtor or enter the premises of the debtor.

555. The basis of enforcement is the execution title, which is usually a decision or a judgment of a court. The most usual judgments in enforcement concern payment obligations. Equally, a judgment that obliges a transfer of the possession of a

14. Proposal for the Enforcement Code and the laws on enforcement of taxes and other public fees HE 83:2006. The Code consolidated following reforms: the organization of enforcement and the judicial review in 1996 (Enforcement Act of 1895 *Ulosottolaki* Chs 1, 9 and 10; 197/1996), the reform of the execution titles and the execution procedure in 2003 (Chs 3, 4 and 6a; 679/2003) and execution, realization of assets and the division of money among the creditors (Chs 4–6; 469/2006).

tangible property can be enforced. In paragraphs 556-562 only the enforcement of these types of judgments are discussed.

556. Also, judgments that oblige a person to do something, to restrain from doing something or to allow another person to do something are enforced according to the Enforcement Code, usually with the threat of a fine (Enforcement Code, Chapter 7). An arbitration award can be enforced according to the Enforcement Code after the district court has given an exequatur in a summary proceeding. The enforcement of a judgment on the custody of a child is regulated in the Act on the Enforcement of a Custody Decision. The enforcement of tax obligations and other obligations of a public law nature are enforced according to the Enforcement of Taxes and Payments Act. Typically, the execution title for the taxes and other public law payments can be a decision of the competent administrative authority and, thus, a court decision or judgment is not required in these cases. The payment of fines is regulated in the Law on the Enforcement of Fines (*Laki sakon täytäntöönpanosta* 672/2002). The competent enforcement authority according to all above-mentioned laws is the enforcement authority. These special procedures are not observed in the following presentation.

557. The enforcement is generally allowed even if the execution title has not obtained res judicata (UK 2:4–12). The debtor can, however, prevent enforcement by putting up collateral for the debt. Even in the absence of such collateral, the enforcement of a monetary judgment cannot be completed, that is, the seized items cannot be sold nor can money be paid to the creditor before the judgment obtains res judicata (UK 2:5). If the seized items quickly lose their value or are expensive to store, they can be sold before the judgment obtains res judicata if the creditor puts up collateral for the repayment and expenses.

558. The creditor files for enforcement to the execution officer either in writing or through an electronic application (UK 3:1). The creditor can file with any execution officer in the country. The competences of the regional execution officers are regulated in a degree of the government (865/2007). As a general rule, the execution officer in the area where the debtor has domicile is competent to handle all enforcement matters against the debtor with the help of execution officers in other places where the debtor has property (UK 3:13–17).

559. The execution starts with a notice to the debtor (UK 3:33). Before that, the execution officer may secure enforcement by interim measures, such as seizure or freezing a bank account, for the maximum period of three weeks (UK 3:18–20). A possibility to grant the debtor time for voluntary payment or a payment plan instead of wage garnishment are regulated in UK 4:60.

560. The law regulates the actions of the execution officer and the officer acts ex officio, so the debtor and the creditor have only limited powers to agree on the execution procedure. Such possibilities to agree on the execution procedure were somewhat widened in the 2003 reform, including a general duty for the execution officer to promote amiable settlements between the parties (UK 1:19; see further

Havansi, 2009; Linna 2008; Linna & Leppänen 2014; Koulu & Lindfors 2009). More specifically, the execution officer has the duty to search for the assets of the debtor, unless the creditor wishes that the execution be limited to the wages or other regular income and the tax returns of the debtor (UK 3:48). The execution officer's coercive powers are regulated in UK 3:49–51 and 3:82–83. The debtor, third parties and authorities are liable to give the execution officer all the relevant information about the economic situation of the debtor (UK 3:52–67).

561. The execution officer can make various legal decisions during the enforcement process, such as defining the sum that is garnished or deciding that an item can or cannot be repossessed when a third party has claimed that the item belongs to him instead of to the debtor. The most important decisions are made in writing (UK 3:28–31). Especially when a claim made by a party or a third party is dismissed and the claim is unclear, the decision is made in writing.

562. The debtor's assets can be repossessed. The assets that the debtor and his family need for their normal everyday life, the tools and educational materials (the *beneficium*) are protected from execution. Also, items comparable with tools, such as cars to go to work, can be exempted from repossession if their value is not unreasonably high or if the debtor can use them to pay off the debt (UK 4:21). The sale of seized property is regulated in UK Chapter 5 and the division of the sale price in Chapter 6.

563. The most common means of enforcement is garnishment of the wages. The employer is notified of the garnishment and becomes liable to turn over the garnished sum to the enforcement authority. General rule for garnishment is that two-thirds of the wages are protected against garnishment; with more complex rules for low and high wages (UK 4:49). A certain minimum income (approximately EUR 600) is always protected against garnishment. Above that income, a progressive scale is applied (UL 4:49).

II. Judicial Review

564. The parties have three main recourses at their disposal: the request to self-correction by the execution officer, the appeal to the district court and the filing of an enforcement dispute in the district court. As most decisions made during the enforcement process can be appealed separately, several legal processes can be pending at the same time. In addition to the debtor and the creditor, also a third party claiming that his property has been repossessed, the buyer of the repossessed property or another creditor can seek recourse.

565. The execution officer can correct computation or typing errors and other obvious mistakes. The execution officer can make a self-correction on his own initiative or after a request by a party (UK 10:1–5).

566. An appeal to the district court must be made within three weeks after the decision was made. An appeal against garnishment of wages is not subject to a time limitation as long as the order given to the employer is in force (UK 11:5). The appeal is handled as an application matter according to Chapter 8 of the Code of Procedure. The competent courts are fourteen specified district courts (UK 11:2.2).

567. An enforcement dispute in the district court is the right legal remedy, for example, when a third party claims that his assets have been repossessed for the debtor's debt (UK 10:6). Especially if the ownership or other right is disputed on evidentiary grounds and the claimant has presented reasonable grounds to support the claim, the dispute cannot be decided in the enforcement procedure and the execution officer should give an instruction to file an enforcement dispute in the district court.

568. The decisions of the district court in appeals and in enforcement disputes can be normally appealed to the appeal court and, subject to leave, to the Supreme Court.

§2. Recognition and Enforcement of Foreign Judgments

I. Rules Applicable in the Absence of a Treaty

569. In the absence of a treaty, a foreign judgment cannot be enforced in Finland. On the other hand, such a foreign judgment has no res judicata-effect in Finland and does not preclude a new trial in a Finnish court. In such a trial, the foreign judgment can have a notable evidentiary value.

570. The most important exception to the above-mentioned rule is the enforcement of international arbitration awards, which are enforceable according to the Arbitration Act §§ 52–55. The system is based on the Convention of 1958 but it covers all international arbitration awards that fulfil the requirements of the Arbitration Act (see Part X, Chapter 8).

571. In addition, it should be mentioned that a divorce granted in a foreign country is generally recognized in Finland (Marriage Act § 121).

II. International Treaties and European Law

572. As a member of the EU, Finland is bound by the Brussels I Regulation (44/2001) since 2002, which has been replaced by Regulation 1215/2012 on jurisdiction and the recognition and enforcement of judgments in civil and commercial matters (recast) since 10 January 2015. Also the Regulation (EC) No. 805/2004 of the European Parliament and of the Council of 21 April 2004 creating a European Enforcement Order for uncontested claims is implemented in Finland.

573. The Nordic Convention on the Recognition and Enforcement of the Civil Judgments (11 October 1977) has become largely obsolete due to European Conventions and Degrees.

574. In matters of family law, the Brussels IIa Decree (2201/2003) on divorce and custody of children: Council Regulation (EC) No. 2201/2003 of 27 November 2003 concerning jurisdiction and the recognition and enforcement of judgments in matrimonial matters and the matters of parental responsibility, repealing Regulation (EC) No. 1347/2000.

575. Finland is party to several international conventions according to which foreign judgments concerning family law are recognized and enforced in Finland. Especially, the rights of children are subject to several international conventions. For example, Finland is party to the Hague Convention on the Recognition and Enforcement of Decisions relating to Maintenance Obligations of 1973 (Law 370/1983), the Hague Convention of 25 October 1980 on the Civil Aspects of International Child Abduction (Child Custody Act, Chapters 5 and 6) and the Hague Convention on Protection of Children and Co-operation in respect of Intercountry Adoption of 29 May 1993 (Adoption Act, Chapter 9).

576. The Nordic conventions in the field of family law still have some importance. There is the Nordic Convention on the Maintenance of 23 March 1962 (Law 702/1962), the Nordic Convention on the Enforcement of the Custody Decisions (Law 761/1970) and the Convention and the Law on the Recognition of Nordic Decisions on Paternity (Law 352/1980). One of the oldest conventions, the Nordic Convention on Marriage, Adoption and Custody of 6 February 1931 (Law 413/1931) is still in force in spite of the Brussels IIa Decree between Finland and Sweden according to the proclamations of both countries.

Part X. Arbitration

Chapter 1. Arbitrability

577. The Arbitration Act of 1992 replaced the old Act on Arbitration of 1928. The act has been drafted in accordance with the principles of UNCITRAL Model Law on Commercial Arbitration. Finland is also party to the New York Convention on the Recognition and Enforcement of Foreign Arbitral Awards of 1958 (Law 200/1962).

578. The Arbitration Act covers both arbitration procedures that are meant to take place in Finland (ArbA §§ 2–50) and the effects of foreign arbitral awards in Finland (ArbA §§ 51–55; about arbitration in Finland see Kurkela 2004; Kurkela & Uoti 1994). By arbitration that is to take place in Finland is meant that the procedural seat of the arbitration is Finland, notwithstanding where the actual hearings are held. The State of the procedural seat is usually defined in the arbitration agreement and the arbitration award should mention the seat of arbitration (ArbA § 36.2). There are a number of provisions in other laws concerning arbitration of specific issues, such as Limited Liability Companies Act (18:3–10).

579. The Arbitration Institute of the Finland Chamber of Commerce (FAI) revised its arbitration rules and rules for expedited arbitration in 2013. It is not unusual that contract partners refer to these rules in a contractual arbitration clause (http://arbitration.fi/arbitration/rules/arbitration-rules/).

580. The arbitration can concern a dispute in a civil or commercial matter, which can be settled by an agreement between the parties (ArbA § 2). Thus, most family law matters, public law matters and criminal matters fall outside the scope of this application. However, arbitration over the compensation of damage caused by a criminal act is possible (KKO:2008:102). Matters of inheritance can be subject to arbitration as well as certain matters of immaterial property law.

581. There are certain provisions on obligatory arbitration procedures, such as arbitration on redemption of shares in a limited liability company or co-operative (Limited Liability Companies Act 16:13; 17:3; 18:3 and 24:4; Co-operatives Act (*Osuuskuntalaki* 421/2013) 26:4).

582. The Consumer Protection Act 12:1d stipulates that an arbitration clause between a consumer and an entrepreneur, which was made before the dispute arose, does not bind the consumer party to the agreement.

Chapter 2. Arbitration Agreement

583. The arbitration agreement can concern a dispute between parties or future disputes between parties that relate to a certain legal relationship or matter.

584. The arbitration agreement is in writing, either in one document or in an exchange of documents between the parties signed by the parties (ArbA § 3). Such a document can also refer to another document containing the arbitration clause. A valid arbitration clause can also be included in a will, a deed of a gift, a bill of lading or similar documents, in the by-laws of an association, foundation, limited-liability company (Limited Liability Companies Act 24:3; Limited Liability Housing Companies Act (*Asunto-osakeyhtiölaki* 1599/2009) 26:3) or of another company (Co-operatives Act 26:3) or corporate entity binding to the parties or to the person against whom a claim is made (ArbA § 4).

585. The validity of the arbitration clause is determined independently from the validity of the contract in which the arbitration clause is included (the doctrine of separability). Even if the contract is deemed invalid or is terminated, the arbitration clause can still be valid. Thus, the arbitrators have generally the jurisdiction to adjudicate on the validity of the contract itself. The arbitrators do not have the final jurisdiction over the validity of the arbitration clause (KKO:1983 II 50; Kurkela & Uoti, 1994, 8–10).

Chapter 3. Arbitration Tribunal

586. The arbitrators are natural persons with full legal capacity. The parties can agree on the qualifications, person and number of the arbitrators. There are three arbitrators unless the parties have agreed on another number (ArbA § 7). The number is even if the parties so agree (Kurkela & Uoti, 20). The arbitrators can be of another nationality than Finnish (ArbA § 8).

587. The arbitration clause either nominates the arbitrators or stipulates the procedure for their appointment. If there is no agreement, each party appoints one (or more) arbitrator and those nominated by the parties appoint the chair (ArbA § 13). If a party does not fulfil his obligations regarding the appointment, the court appoints the arbitrator (ArbA § 15).

588. The rules of the Finnish Arbitration Institute include detailed rules for appointing the arbitrator or arbitrators for both situations in which the parties can agree on the arbitrator(s) and in which they are not able agree (rules 15-19). In disagreement, the board of the institute appoints the arbitrator. The default rule is that only one arbitrator is appointed if the interest and other traits of the dispute do not require the appointment of three arbitrators. The procedure for appointing the arbitrator(s) can be followed even if the rules are not otherwise followed.

589. The arbitrators are impartial and independent. The arbitrator discloses any circumstances that can raise doubts as to his impartiality (ArbA § 9). If the arbitrator is disqualified to act as a judge in the matter or if his impartiality is questionable on some other ground, a party can challenge the arbitrator. The parties can agree on the procedure in which the challenge is handled. If not otherwise agreed, the challenge is made to the arbitration tribunal within fifteen days from the time when the party became aware of the circumstances endangering the impartiality of the arbitrator (ArbA § 11). According to ArbA § 41, disqualification of an arbitrator is a ground for setting aside an arbitral award.

590. The arbitrators decide the seat of arbitration if it is not decided in the arbitration agreement (ArbA § 24). The actual proceedings can be carried out in another place as well, even in another country.

Chapter 4. Interim Measures and Preliminary Awards

591. The interim measures regulated in Code of Procedure Chapter 7 can be granted by the district court in advance of an arbitration procedure. In such a situation, the arbitration must be initiated within one month from the district court's decision.

592. According to the rules of the Arbitration Institute, also the arbitration tribunal can give interim measures of protection and require a security for those (rule 36). For urgent situations, there are also rules for emergency arbitrator. Such emergency arbitrator can be appointed before the appointment procedure for arbitrators has been completed (Appendix III of the FAI rules).

593. As a different procedure, the arbitration tribunal can also issue a separate arbitration award on any issue which is preliminary in relation to the final award (ArbA 35).

Chapter 5. Conduct of Arbitral Proceedings

594. The arbitration clause hands the jurisdiction over the dispute to the arbitration tribunal. If a dispute is brought to a court, the defendant invokes the arbitration clause at the time of submitting his first statement on the substance of the dispute and the court dismisses the case (ArbA § 5.1). If the defendant does not raise the objection and invoke the arbitration agreement, the defendant is deemed to have accepted the jurisdiction of the district court. If the other party subverts the arbitration by not nominating an arbitrator or by refusing to pay the costs, a party can also bring the case to court (ArbA § 6).

595. The arbitration is instigated by notifying the other party of the intention to submit a dispute to arbitration and of the appointment of an arbitrator by the party (ArbA §§ 12 and 21).

596. The parties have the discretion to agree on the procedural rules to be followed. If such an agreement is lacking, the arbitrators decide on the appropriate conduct of the proceedings (ArbA § 23; see also § 25), on the language used (ArbA § 26), on calling in an expert (ArbA § 28), etc.

597. There are some fundamental principles of due process that must be respected. First, both parties are given a sufficient opportunity to present their case (ArbA § 22). They have the right to present their grounds and evidence, hear and comment on the arguments of the other party and to hear and question evidence put forward by the other party (KKO:2008:77). The parties must be given a fair opportunity to do this but they are not obliged to actively pursue their claims.

598. The district court has certain 'supporting' jurisdiction in arbitration. First, the district court can grant interim protective measures before and during the arbitration (ArbA § 5.2; see Part IX, Chapter 1). Such measures do not fall within the jurisdiction of the arbitration tribunal. Second, the arbitration tribunal can refer a hearing of a witness or the disclosure of a document to the district court that can hear the witness under affirmation of truth or can order the deposition of a document (ArbA § 29).

Chapter 6. Arbitral Award

599. The arbitration award is based on the law. The parties can, however, entrust the arbitrators to decide the case on the basis of equity; that is *ex aeque et bono* (ArbA § 31).

600. The parties can agree that the arbitration tribunal applies the law of a certain state when deciding on the matter of the dispute (ArbA § 31.2). In practice, the parties can also agree that the dispute is decided on the basis of *lex mercatoria*, international commercial law and practice (Kurkela & Uoti, 63). In the absence of such an agreement, the rules of international private law are followed.

601. If the parties reach a settlement in the dispute during the arbitration, they can submit the settlement to the arbitration tribunal for confirmation (ArbA § 33), which has the same legal effect as an arbitration award. The formal requirements for the arbitration award are regulated in ArbA § 36.

602. The enforcement of the arbitral award is sought from the district court that issues an exequatur (ArbA § 43). The losing party is heard before the exequatur is issued unless there is a particular obstacle to it. The enforcement is carried out by the enforcement agencies.

Chapter 7. Recourse Against Arbitral Award

603. The arbitration tribunal has limited jurisdiction to correct the award within a short time lime in accordance with ArbA § 38. Thus, the tribunal can correct a typing or computation error or another error of similar nature. The request for the correction must be made within thirty days after the party received the award. The arbitrators can also correct such an error on their own initiative within thirty days. The arbitrators can also, after a request from a party, complete the award on an issue that was omitted from the award (ArbA § 39).

604. There is no ordinary appeal against the arbitration award. The parties can, however, seek the reversal of the award in the district court in the area of the venue of the arbitration (ArbA §§ 50 and 36.2; about the venue in arbitration according to the Limited Liability Companies Act see KKO:2010:10) by invoking the grounds mentioned in ArbA § 41. In addition, an arbitration award can be null and void, in which case no action is needed (ArbA § 40). The nullity of the award can, in principle, be recognized, for example, in the enforcement process (ArbA § 44).

605. The grounds for nullity are enumerated in ArbA § 40, according to which the arbitration award can be null and void under four circumstances. First, if the award adjudicates a matter excluded from arbitration according to Finnish law, such as a criminal matter or custody of children, it is null and void. Second, an award in conflict with the foundations of the Finnish legal order is null and void. Thus, it is not enough that the award can be an object of legal critique but it has to be contradictory to quite fundamental public policies. Third, an award that is so incomplete or obscure that it does not disclose what has been decided is null and void. This ground is similar to OK 31:1.1 point 4 concerning extraordinary review of judgments. Fourth, an award that is not signed by the arbitrators according to ArbA § 36 is null and void. An arbitrator cannot, however, disrupt the procedure by withholding his signature; the other arbitrators can complete the award by a note on the missing signature in such a case.

606. The four grounds for reversal are enumerated in ArbA § 41. These grounds are procedural in nature. There is no requirement that the error actually affected the content of the award.

607. First, the arbitration award can be reversed if the arbitrators exceeded their authority. The main source of the authority of the arbitrators is, of course, the arbitration agreement. If they exceed its boundaries, the award can for that part be reversed. Similarly, the arbitrators are limited by the actions of the parties and cannot adjudicate a matter not brought to them for adjudication (see KKO:2008:77, 11–13).

608. Second, the award can be reversed if the arbitrators have not been appointed in due order or an arbitrator should have been disqualified. The procedures for appointing an arbitrator are regulated in ArbA §§ 12–19. If an arbitrator is

to be disqualified, a party has to make an objection about it to the arbitration tribunal. If the objection does not lead to the disqualification or if the party becomes aware of the ground for disqualification too late to make such an objection, that party can seek reversal of the arbitration award.

609. It is possible that the party waives the right to seek the reversal of the award on the above-mentioned grounds (ArbA § 41.2).

610. Third, an arbitration award can be reversed if the tribunal has not given the parties a fair opportunity to pursue their case (ArbA § 41.1, 4). It is required that the proceedings follow the fundamental principles of due process and allow the parties to present their case and evidence and to contest the claims and evidence of the party. There are, however, no set rules for how the proceeding should be organized, except for the general principles set out in ArbA § 25 (see KKO:2008:77).

Chapter 8. Recognition and Enforcement of Arbitral Awards

611. Since 1962 Finland is a party to the New York Convention on the Recognition and Enforcement of Foreign Arbitral Awards (10 June 1958). Arbitration Act §§ 51– 55 regulate the recognition and the enforcement of international arbitration awards in Finland. These provisions have been enacted to a large extent to correspond to the provisions of the convention.

612. An international arbitration clause can be invoked in a Finnish court as an impediment to the Finnish proceedings. A defendant must make such an objection before answering to the main action (ArbA § 51). The international arbitration clause should, however, be concluded according to the provisions of ArbA §§ 3 and 4. Notwithstanding such an agreement or such proceedings, the Finnish courts can grant interim measures.

613. A foreign arbitration award is, in principle, recognized and enforced in Finland in the same way as a domestic arbitration award. It is required that the arbitration agreement is made according to the principles mentioned in the ArbA §§ 3 and 4. The exequatur is given by the district court (ArbA § 54). The application for an exequatur must be accompanied by the award, the arbitration agreement or validated copies and a translation in the Finnish or Swedish language unless the court agrees that a translation is unnecessary. The opposing party is heard before the exequatur is given, unless there is a specific objection to it.

614. A foreign arbitration award is not, however, valid in Finland if it is in conflict with the fundamental principles of the Finnish legal order. Such invalidity does not require an action from a party (ArbA § 51.2).

615. A party can invoke the invalidity of an arbitration award on the grounds enumerated in ArbA § 53. First, a party can object to the validity of the arbitration agreement. The invalidity of the arbitration agreement depends on a number of grounds, for example, that the party had no competence to conclude it or was not duly represented at the conclusion of such an agreement. The invalidity of the agreement can also be due to another reason, with the exception of a purely formal reason, according to the law of the country the parties have chosen or according to the law of the country in which the award was given.

616. Second, the party can invoke a procedural objection to the validity of the arbitration award. Such an objection can be based on the fact the party was not given due notice of the appointment of the arbitrator or the proceedings. A procedural objection can also be that a party was not given appropriate opportunity to present his/her case or that the proceedings deviated otherwise from what was agreed or required according to the law of the arbitration. In addition, the validity can depend on the arbitrators exceeding their authority or that the arbitration tribunal has not fulfilled the requirements of the agreement or the relevant law.

617. Finally, an arbitration award is not in force in Finland when it is not binding in the country in which it was given, or if its enforceability was postponed in that country or if it was reversed.

Part XI. Mediation

Chapter 1. Legislation/Definitions

618. A distinction must be made between four types of mediation: (1) court led mediation in civil matters, (2) mediation in criminal and civil matters under the municipal mediation offices, (3) mediation by the social services in child custody matters and (4) mediation programs by NGOs. In this Part XI court led mediation according to the CivMedAct is explained in detail. First, however, the scope of the four types of mediation is explained (Chapter 1).

619. Court led mediation is regulated in the Act on Mediation in Civil Matters and Confirmation of Settlements in General Courts (CivMedAct; *Laki riita-asioiden sovittelusta ja sovinnon vahvistamisesta yleisissä tuomioistuimissa* 394/2011), which has replaced CivMedAct 663/2005. The court led mediation was not particularly popular in the beginning. In the early 2010s, an experimental project on mediation of custody disputes between parents was started. After a trial period in some district courts, mediation of custody disputes has become a standard procedure according to changes to CivMedAct in 2014 (316/2014).

620. Another mediation procedure is regulated in the Act on Conciliation in Criminal and Certain Civil Cases (Conciliation Act *Laki rikosasioiden ja eräiden riitä-asioiden sovittelusta* 1015/2005). The scope of this Act covers, besides criminal matters and compensation claims related to crime, also civil claims, in which at least one of the parties is a natural person and which are of minor nature (§ 1.2). According to this Act, the municipalities are obliged to offer mediation services either through their own mediation offices or through another service provider. Usually several municipalities provide the service together. Actual mediation is carried out by lay mediators who are trained for this service.

621. A conciliation agreement does not prevent the prosecutor from bringing charges, but according to the Criminal Procedure Act (ROL 1:8.1 point 1) a conciliation agreement and even a genuine attempt to achieve conciliation is one of the grounds, on which the prosecutor may drop charges. It has to be noted here that a conciliation agreement on the compensation cannot be enforced by the enforcement agent. Since the mediation according to Conciliation Act is mostly directed towards criminal offences and compensation claims, it is not further discussed here.

622. Since 1998, the Finnish Bar Association has offered a mediation program, accepted rules of mediation and educated its members to act as mediators. The mediation is confidential and its costs are divided equally between the parties. The program has not been very popular so far and only a few disputes have been settled through mediation (the rules and a standard contract can be found at www.asiana-jajat.fi).

623. In disputes over custody of children between the parents, several municipal authorities and non-governmental organizations offer mediation services. The municipal social services have an authority to confirm a settlement on custody, visitation rights and alimony payments and these settlements can be enforced (see Part IX, Chapter 2). Circa 90% of child custody matters are agreed and the social services confirm the settlement. In principle, parents can agree and bring the agreement to the court as well but the social services are the preferred option.

Chapter 2. Rights That Can be Subject to Mediation

624. According to CivMedAct §1 all civil disputes can be mediated. Thus, all civil and commercial disputes can be mediated. The scope of the law covers also civil claims on compensation based on a criminal offence. The scope of the law is not limited to dispositive matters but covers also indispositive civil matters, including disputes over custody of children, right to visitation and alimony to children.

625. In addition, the matter should be suitable to mediation and the mediation should be appropriate when the claims of the parties are taken into account (§ 3). Thus, if there is no possibility to settle the case, it should go directly to trial.

626. Settlements that are achieved in the procedure according to the CivMedAct can be enforced by the enforcement agent in the same way as civil judgments. The CivMedAct also regulates the procedure, in which an out-of-court settlement can be confirmed by a court so that it can be enforced.

Chapter 3. Mediation Application and Agreement

627. The court led mediation starts with an application to the district court by either both or one of the parties (§ 4). The rules on jurisdiction equal those of a civil procedure (§ 11). The application is made in writing. Basically, the same formalities are followed as in the application for summons, though less formally.

628. An application for mediation can also be made while a civil case is pending in the court. Such an application must be made during the preparatory stage of the trial.

629. Both parties must agree to mediation. If they do not apply for the appointment of a mediator together, the other party is heard either orally in front of a judge or in writing (§ 4).

630. The decision to commence a mediation procedure and to nominate a mediator cannot be appealed (§ 17).

Chapter 4. Persons/Institutions That Can Act as Mediator

631. The mediator in the CivMedAct-procedure is a district court judge. An interesting difference to any other court proceedings is that the parties may wish for a named judge to become the mediator. That wish cannot always be fulfilled but even the possibility to express such wish is exceptional.

632. The mediator may have an expert to aid him/her. Such an expert is nominated by the mediator herself after a consultation and agreement of the parties. The idea is that while the judge stands for the mediation and adjudication skills, the expert should bring in the knowledge of substance of the matter. The parties pay the remuneration for the expert.

633. In child custody disputes the expert must be a psychologist, a psychiatrist or a social worker according to the Child Custody Act §§ 17b and 17c. In these matters the expert's expenses and fee are paid by the state.

634. The mediator and the expert have the obligation of confidentiality, which can be broken by the court or by a legal provision (§ 15).

Chapter 5. Mediation Procedure

635. The purpose of mediation is to aid the parties in finding an amicable settlement to their dispute. The mediator has considerable discretion in how to organize the procedure. The mediator must hear the parties, and even if a settlement can be reached on the documents, usually at least one hearing in the court is organized. The hearing is often held quite soon after the commencement of the proceedings. In child dispute cases where a special rule requires that the hearing is organized without delay (§10), the average time in custody mediation has been 1.5 months. There is no rule as to how long the meetings should be, but they usually take 1–2 hours.

636. The parties have a considerable influence on how the mediation procedure is organized. With the consent of both parties, the mediator may allow that documentary evidence is presented or that other persons than the parties are heard. If the parties agree, the mediator can negotiate with each of the parties without the presence of the other party. Finally, if the parties request or allow, the mediator can make a settlement proposal (§§ 7–8).

637. The parties may have attorneys present during the mediation, and they also may get legal aid. The qualifications for the assistance of a party are, however, much more flexible than in regular civil proceedings (§ 15). Both parties are responsible for their own costs in mediation (§ 27).

638. If the mediator comes to the conclusion that a settlement cannot be reached, the mediator shall terminate the procedure. If the matter is pending as a civil trial, the civil procedure shall continue. The judge, who has acted as mediator, may not adjudicate the case.

639. As a starting point, mediation is not more or less confidential than ordinary civil procedure. However, a conversation between the judge and one of the parties can be held in private. Also if the parties request and present a valid reason for it, the judge may order that the public has no access to the mediation hearings. (CivMedAct § 12). The parties cannot invoke a concession made by the other party in the mediation in a later trial or other procedure concerning the dispute (CivMedAct § 13).

Chapter 6. Settlement Agreement

640. When a settlement is reached, it is confirmed by the court. Thus, it has the same res judicata effect as settlement confirmed during the trial, and basically the same effect as a judgment. A confirmed settlement can be enforced by the enforcement agent, for example.

641. The settlement is not bound by the strict rules of preclusion and the limits of the case. If the parties so agree, the settlement can cover issues that were not included in the initial application for the mediation procedure (§ 8).

642. In child custody cases, the mediator has a special duty to supervise that the settlement fulfils the requirements of the Child Custody Act and Act on the Maintenance of a Child and to protect the best interest of the child.

Chapter 7. Setting Aside a Settlement Agreement

643. There is a right of appeal to the decision of the court to confirm a settlement (OK 20:5). It is also possible to bring a case and argue that a settlement was reached using methods that make a contract invalid according to the Contracts Act (228/1929; KKO:2012:35). Whether a settlement was reached or not, the parties are not allowed to plead the submissions or other statements made in the mediation in a subsequent trial (§ 16).

Chapter 8. International Mediation

644. CivMedAct Chapter 3 regulates the confirmation of a settlement that has been negotiated out-of-court. At the request of both parties to the settlement, the court can confirm the settlement and it will acquire res judicata effect and become enforceable. The confirmation procedure can be applied to dispositive civil and commercial disputes, including settlements that are made in another country according to the Directive 2008/52/EC of the European Parliament and of the Council on certain aspects of mediation in civil and commercial matters.

The confirmation of an agreement on child custody, visitation rights or alimony cannot be confirmed according to CivMedAct.

Selected Bibliography

§1. In English

Autio, A-L. 'The Main Problems in Access to Court Regarding the Dispute Resolution of Finnish Companies' In *The Future of Civil Litigation: Access to Courts and Court-annexed Mediation in the Nordic Countries*, Laura Ervo, Anna Nylund, editors. Cham: Springer, 2014. 213–231.

Aarnio, A. Reason and Authority: A Treatise on the Dynamic Paradigm of Legal Reasoning. Aldershot, 1997.

Ervasti, K. 'Court-Connected Meditation in Finland: Experiences' In *The Future of Civil Litigation: Access to Courts and Court-annexed Mediation in the Nordic Countries*, Laura Ervo, Anna Nylund, editors. Cham: Springer, 2014. 121–137.

Ervo, L. (ed.). *Civil Justice in Finland.* Jikakusha, 2009.

Ervo, L. 'Class Actions – Scandinavian Novelties'. In *Current Topics of International Litigation*, edited by R. Stürner & M. Kawano. Tübingen: Mohr Siebeck, 2009.

Ervo, L. 'Order for Payment in Finland'. In *Orders for Payment in the European Union*, edited by W.H. Rechberger & G.E. Kodek. The Hague: Kluwer Law International, 2001, 121–129.

Ervo, L. 'The Principle of the Free Reception of Evidence in Finland'. In *Proceedings of the First World Conference on New Trends in Criminal Investigation and Evidence*, edited by J.F. Nijboer & J.M. Reijntjes. Hauge: Open University of the Netherlands, 1997, 295–299.

Ervo, L. 'The Reform of Civil Procedure in Finland'. *Civil Justice Quarterly* 14 (1995): 56–64.

Hollo, E. (ed.). *Finnish legal system and recent development.* Helsinki: Edita, 2006.

Jokela, A. 'Legal Procedure'. In *An Introduction to Finnish Law*, edited by Juha Pöyhönen. 2nd rev. ed. Helsinki: Finnish Lawyer's Publishing, 2002, 357–402.

Klami, H.T., M. Gräns & J. Sorvettula. *Law and Truth. A Theory of Evidence.* Finnish Society of Sciences and Letters, 2000.

Kurkela, M.S. & Uoti, P. *Arbitration in Finland.* Helsinki: Finnish Lawyer's Publishing, 1994.

Kurkela, M. 'Due process in arbitration: A Finnish perspective.' *Journal of International Arbitration* 21.2 (2004): 221–225.

Lager, I. 'Civil and Administrative Procedure: The Differences and Their Explanation'. In *The Finnish National Reports to the XIIIth Congress of the International Academy of Comparative Law.* Montreal, 19–24 August 1990/edited by K. Buure-Hägglund, H.E.S. Mattila, K. Kilpeläinen. Hki, 1990, 47–54.

Männistö, Jarkko. *Theory of preclusion.* Helsinki: Ajatuspaja Käräjä 2013.
Niemi-Kiesiläinen, J. 'Efficiency and Justice in Procedural Reforms: The Rise and Fall of the Oral Hearing'. In *Civil Justice between Efficiency and Quality: From Ius Commune to the CEPEJ*, edited by C.H. van Rhee & A. Uzelac. Antwerp: Intersentia, 2008, 29–45.
Nuotio, K. & Melander, S. & Huomo-Kettunen, M. (eds): *Introduction to Finnish law and legal culture.* Forum Iuris, 2012.
Pihlajamäki, H. *Evidence, Crime, and the Legal Profession: The Emergence of Free Evaluation of Evidence in the Finnish Nineteenth-Century Criminal Procedure.* Lund: Institutet för rättshistorisk forskning, 1997.
Pöyhönen, J. *An Introduction to Finnish Law* 2nd rev. ed. Helsinki: Finnish Lawyer's Publishing, 2002.
Rosti H., J. Niemi & M. Lasola. *Legal Aid and Legal Services in Finland.* Helsinki: National Research Institute of Legal Policy, 2008.
Suviranta, O. 'Compensation for a Public Service Not Received: A Dual/Parallel Competence of Finnish Ordinary and Administrative Courts of Law?'. In *Parallel and Conflicting Enforcement of Law*, edited by Torbjörn Andersson. Stockholm: Norstedts/Martinus Nijhoff, 2005.
Vilkkonen, E. 'Court Organization and Procedure'. In *The Finnish Legal System*, edited by Jaakko Uotila. 2nd Compl. revised edn. Helsinki: Finnish Lawyers Publishing Company, 1985, 90–100.

§2. In Finnish

Ervasti, K. 'Riita-asiat tuomioistuimissa'. In Oikeusolot, edited by Marjukka Lasola. *Oikeuspoliittisen tutkimuslaitoksen julkaisuja 244/2009*, p. 43–64.
Ervo, L. *Oikeudenmukainen oikeudenkäynti.* WSOY, 2005.
Frände, D., et al. *Prosessioikeus.* Sanoma Pro, 2012.
Halila, J. *Todistustaakan jaosta silmällä pitäen erityisesti varallisuusoikeudellisia oikeussuhteita.* Suomalainen lakimiesyhdistys, 1955.
Haapasalo, J., Kiesiläinen, K., Niemi–Kiesiläinen, J. *Todistajan psykologia ja todistajankuulustelu.* Lakimiesliiton kustannus, 2000.
Havansi, E. 'Ulosotto–oikeus'. In *Insolvenssioikeus*, edited by Koulu et al.WSOY, 2005.
Hepola, M. *Oikeusvoimaopin transformaatio. Siviiliprosessioikeudellisen oikeusvoimaopin muuttuminen ja siirtyminen hallinto – ja ympäristöoikeuteen ympäristöluvan pysyvyyden kannalta.* Edilex, 2005.
Huovila, M. *Periaatteet ja perustelut: tutkimus käräjäoikeuden tuomion faktaperusteluista prosessuaalisten periaatteiden valossa arvioituna.* Suomalainen lakimiesyhdistys, 2003.
Jokela, A. *Oikeudenkäynti III*, Talentum 2005.
Jokela, A. *Hovioikeusmenettely.* Talentum 2010.
Jokela, A. *Oikeudenkäynnin asianosaiset ja valmistelu – Oikeudenäynti II.* Talentum 2012.
Jonkka, J. Syytekynnys. *Tutkimus syytteen nostamiseen tarvittavan näytön arvioinnista.* Suomalainen lakimiesyhdistys, 1991.

Koulu, R. & Lindfors, H. *Ulosotto-oikeus*. Edita 2009.

Lappalainen, J. *Suomen Siviiliprosessioikeus 1*. WSOY, 1995.

Lappalainen, J. *Suomen Siviiliprosessioikeus 2*. WSOY, 2000.

Lappalainen, J., Todistusoikeus, Tuomion oikeusvoima etc. In Frände et al. *Prosessioikeus*. WSOY, 2012.

Laukkanen, S. *Selvä ja täsmällinen tuomio: selvitys käräjäoikeuden tuomion kirjoittamisesta*. Oikeusministeriö, 2002.

Laukkanen, S. *Tuomarin rooli: prosessioikeudellinen tutkimus tuomarin roolista dispositiivisen riita–asian valmistelussa silmällä pitäen riidan kohteen selvittämistä*. Suomalainen lakimiesyhdistys, 1995.

Leppänen, T. *Riita–asian valmistelu todistusaineiston osalta: prosessioikeudellinen tutkimus*. Suomalainen lakimiesyhdistys, 1998.

Linna, T. *Ulosottokaaren pääkohdat*. Talentum 2008.

Linna, T. & Leppänen T. *Ulosotto-oikeus I. Ulosottomenettely*. Talentum 2014.

Niemi J., H. Väkiparta & H. Tarkkala. *Asiamieskielto ja perimiskulut*. National Research Institute of Legal Policy, 2009.

Nylund, A. *Tillgången till den andra instansen i tvistemål*. Suomalainen lakimiesyhdistys, 2006.

Saranpää, T. *Näyttöenemmyysperiaate riita-asiassa*. Suomalainen lakimiesyhdistys 2010.

Tirkkonen, T. *Suomen Siviiliprosessioikeus I*. 2p. WSOY, 1974.

Tirkkonen, T. *Suomen Siviiliprosessioikeus II*. 2p. WSOY, 1977.

Vaitoja, J. *Väittämistaakka, tuomarin kyselyvelvollisuus ja pakottavaan yksityisoikeudelliseen sääntelyyn perustuvien vaatimusten tutkiminen siviiliprosessissa*. Suomalainen lakimiesyhdistys, 2014.

Virolainen, J. & P. Martikainen. *Pro & Contra: tuomion perustelemisen keskeisiä kysymyksiä*. Talentum, 2003.

Selected Bibliography

Index

The numbers here refer to paragraph numbers

Index

Made in the USA
Monee, IL
18 October 2026

66037586R10096